Advance Praise for
The Top Ten Operational Risks

"Investment operations can be complex, and yet the back office is often overlooked. The authors explain the risks and provide clear guidance for best practices."

—**Bill Bogle**
Partner and Chief Compliance Officer, NEPC LLC

"In the wake of the global financial crisis, asset management firms are paying more attention, not only to investment risk management, but also to oversight of the operational risks that come with day-to-day activities like portfolio valuation. Stone House Consulting's book contains timely and thought-provoking essays of current interest to operations and technology managers."

—**Bruce J. Feibel**, CFA
Managing Director, BNY Mellon

"Readers will appreciate the pragmatic, forward-looking approach adopted in this book. When discussing issues like automation, outsourcing or accounting that practitioners encounter in their daily work, the authors' aim is always to show how risk tools may prevent problems from occurring."

—**Jacques Gagné**, CFA, CIPM, FSA
asset and risk manager, Québec

"Anyone working in a managerial or supervisory capacity in the investment industry would do well to secure a copy of Stone House Consulting's book on operational risk. The writing is concise, the content is relevant, and the guidance is realistic. You will have immediate take-away value."

—**Sandra Hahn-Colbert**, CFA
Managing Director and Director, Performance, Risk & Operations,
O'Shaughnessy Asset Management

Advance Praise

"*The Top Ten Operational Risks* is a must-read for Chief Compliance Officers. Substitute 'compliance' for 'operations' and you have an outline of how build a proactive Compliance Program designed to consistently and effectively prevent, detect, and correct compliance problems, while efficiently utilizing your firm's resources."

—**Bart McDonald**
Executive Vice President and Chief Operating Officer
Renaissance Regulatory Services, Inc.

"Here's a checklist of sound operational practices—written in plain English. Use it!"

—**Alan M. Meder**, CFA
Chief Risk Officer, Duff & Phelps Investment Management Co.

"I began my career as an equity assistant and learned the business from the bottom up; for those who were privileged to start out at the top of the process as portfolio managers, these papers should be required reading. *The Top Ten Areas* is a book I want in my office, yesterday, and I'll get additional copies for other members of the firm."

—**Janet T. Miller**, CFA
Partner, Rowland & Company

"When many investors think about risk, they worry that the assets they've bought could go down in value. But that's a risk with an upside—you have to take that risk to make money. Investors must work even more carefully to avoid taking risks that have no upside, which Holly Miller and Philip Lawton categorize as 'operational risks.' Far more firms have been sunk by easily avoidable operational risks than by fluctuations in asset values. These sinkings are a completely unnecessary tragedy. Read Ms. Miller and Mr. Lawton's volume to learn how to avoid them."

—**Laurence B. Siegel**
Research Director, The Research Foundation of CFA Institute

The Top Ten Operational Risks

A Survival Guide for Investment Management Firms and Hedge Funds

Holly H. Miller and Philip Lawton

With a Foreword by Milton Ezrati

© 2010 Stone House Consulting, LLC

All rights reserved. No portion of this book may be reproduced without written permission of the publisher. For information, please contact Stone House Consulting, LLC, 126 Thornton Road, Thornton, PA 19373.

Foreword, Milton Ezrati

Original Articles, Holly H. Miller and Philip Lawton

"Mitigating Lottery Risk," by Philip Lawton was original published in *Performance Measurement and Client Reporting Review*, Vol 3.1, Autumn 2010. Reprinted with permission from Osney Media.

Cover art and book design, Kerry Gibbons

Photograph on page 8, ©iStockphoto.com/VisualField; page 11, ©iStockphoto.com/biffspandex; page 15, ©iStockphoto.com/clearstockconcepts; page 20, ©iStockphoto.com/DOConnell; page 25, ©iStockphoto.com/technotr; page 48, ©iStockphoto.com/mloc; page 54, ©iStockphoto.com/mevans; Original typewriter photo on page 30, ©iStockphoto.com/PhillDanze; Illustration page 37, ©iStockphoto.com/sjlocke; page 42, ©iStockphoto.com/robynmac. Some images have been altered.

Photographs on pages 60 and 64, Holly H. Miller

Photograph on page 66, Philip Lawton

Flow charts on pages 27, 28 and 40, Holly H. Miller

ISBN-13: 978-1456367879

ISBN-10: 1456367870

BISAC: Business & Economics / Investments & Securities

Printed On-Demand from Amazon.com.

Contents

Foreword	*viii*
Preface	*xi*
Introduction	1
Complacency	4
The Blind Leading the Blind	8
Novices, Apprentices and Soloists	13
Dropped Batons	18
Naïve Reliance on Technology	23
Playbooks	30
Amalgamated Assignments	35
Reconciliation Gaps	41
Reading the Fine Print	47
Poor Planning and Slow Response Times	51
Conclusion	58
Appendix: Mitigating Lottery Risk	63
About Stone House Consulting, LLC	68

Foreword

I EMBRACED the opportunity to write this foreword because these essays on operational risk shocked me. A career in investment management and research had acquainted me well with both investment risk and business risk but, I am embarrassed to say, not with all the diverse and nuanced aspects of risk on the operational side of an investment firm. Like so many others in investments, research, marketing, sales and the executive suite, I considered operations more or less cut-and-dried, a place where diligent people did essential tasks in ways that were fairly obvious and, if done with care, carried essentially no risk. As long as all the "i"s were dotted and the "t"s were crossed, I had assumed, all would go smoothly. These essays, as each appeared week by week on the Stone House Consulting website, disabused me of such notions, shaking me out of a complacency of which I was unaware and alerting me to the varied and intricate nature of operational risks.

Few things can unsettle more thoroughly than the discovery that danger lies where one had previously seen security, like finding out that piranhas swim in the river where you have allowed the children to play. The first impulse is denial, then panic, and then, because in this business one cannot avoid operations as one would that river, an intense desire to find a way to lessen the peril. These essays also provide the desired guidance. Unlike so many other articles on problems, they go beyond vivid descriptions of what can go wrong and add direction on how to correct matters and guard against future troubles through well-considered staffing, procedures, technical support and training. In terms of our piscine analogy, they tell not only that there are piranhas in the water but also where they might congregate, how they might be contained and, if necessary, how to sweep them from the river altogether.

This last aspect of these brief articles stands as their greatest virtue, at least where practical men and women are concerned. No general statement, of course, can answer for the specifics of any firm. Different product groupings, different numbers and types of clients, different endowments of human capital and different corporate histories demand very particularized solutions. But the directions offered here will give managers a good idea of what needs to be done and provide them enough material to ask the right questions of their operations people and consultants. It is for this facet of the discussion in particular that I recommend these essays.

Parts of this collection will have a greater or lesser appeal to different managers. Some will see a broad need just from reading the introduction. Some, very probably because of a past mishap, will feel familiar with the difficulties that form the basis of a particular essay and believe, rightly or wrongly, that they have that area covered. Those who nonetheless read on will find that this nuanced material uncovers problems even in common "solutions" and offers ways to correct them.

The order here makes the reading effortless whether it is done from beginning to end or selectively by subject. After the introduction, chapters one through three take up personnel issues, including matters of training and backup. Essays four through seven address organizational and support issues, including a discussion of where technology can help and, remarkably these days, where it can raise problems. The last three essays, numbers eight through ten, focus on particular areas of weakness, reconciliation, legal and planning. Though a helpful packaging of the problems, here as elsewhere matters are interrelated in reality. Accordingly, each discussion necessarily draws on the others and indicates when it is doing so.

For all this, these short essays are an easy, quick read, a merciful quality for busy people in an age of information overload. The investment of an hour or two will offer managers numerous ways to improve their firm and their client service, and, critically, a means to guard against rather large, unexpected expenses.

Milton Ezrati[1]

---

[1] Mr. Ezrati is Partner, Senior Economist and Market Strategist for Lord Abbett & Co. LLC. Among many other publications, Mr. Ezrati is the author of *Kawari: How Japan's Economic and Cultural Transformation Will Alter the Balance of Power Among Nations* (Reading, MA: Perseus Books, 1999). For obvious reasons, Lord Abbett cannot endorse any book or document outside its own publications. Mr. Ezrati writes here in his own capacity as a Wall Street veteran of 40 years.

Preface

CLIENTS suffer when investment management firms and hedge funds fail. We wrote these essays for investment managers, notably including hedge fund managers, but we tried to avoid or explain technical terms in order to make the concepts easily accessible. We earnestly hope traditional and alternative money managers will find this little book valuable in strengthening their operational risk controls. We also hope regulators, institutional investors, family offices, high-net-worth individuals, and others with a stake in the functioning of the capital markets will find it helpful in selecting and monitoring investment managers.

This project originated with a presentation and discussion at a meeting of the DC Metro Area Compliance Roundtable hosted by WTAS LLC in McLean, Virginia. The body of the present work consists of a collection of articles we posted, one each week, on the Stone House Consulting website between 10 August and 18 October 2010. The working title for this series was, "The Top Ten Areas of Buy-Side Operational Risk." We are grateful to the members of the DC Metro Area Compliance Roundtable for their lively interest in the topic and to the readers who commented on various issues and encouraged us to continue writing about operational risk.

The versions contained in this book have been lightly edited. New material includes a foreword, graciously contributed by Milton Ezrati, and a conclusion. We also present a closely related article as an appendix. "Mitigating Lottery Risk" originally appeared in

Performance Measurement and Client Reporting Review, an Osney Media publication expertly edited by Deborah Valentine.

Stone House Consulting, LLC

INTRODUCTION

OPERATIONAL risk is a serious concern not only to traditional and alternative investment managers but also to their clients and the organizations that regulate buy-side firms. In worst-case scenarios, an investment firm's failure to identify and mitigate operational risk can result in significant direct costs and a devastating loss of reputation. It may take years to reassure investors, regulators and trading partners that the firm is well-managed.

So what exactly is operational risk? Castle Hall Alternatives[1] calls it "risk without reward." The Basel Committee on Banking Supervision defines operational risk as "the risk of loss resulting from inadequate or failed internal processes, people and systems or from external events," states that the definition is intended to include legal risk but exclude reputational risk and lists as examples events ranging from data entry errors to earthquakes.[2]

---

[1] castlehallalternatives.com

[2] "Sound Practices for the Management and Supervision of Operational

But operational risk is not something that can be easily identified by a generic checklist, nor is there a single, universally applicable approach to mitigating the operational risks to which a given firm is exposed. Different organizations will have different exposures (depending, for instance, upon their investment strategies, the markets in which they operate and the instruments they employ) as well as varying tolerance levels for operational risk, just as they have with regard to investment risk.

Nonetheless, there are key areas to look for risk within an investment management organization. In addition, there are some straightforward approaches to mitigating operational risk that can be deployed by large and small organizations alike. Many of these approaches will address several key risk areas at once.

In the next ten chapters, Stone House Consulting covers our "top ten" areas of operational risk with a short essay on each one, including suggestions for identifying whether these risks exist within your organization and steps to mitigate them. Although there is no one-size-fits-all solution for operational risk management, we hope these chapters will help many organizations reduce their operational risk profile.

The following "top ten" list summarizes the areas where we most often see operational risk—which is not necessarily where the greatest risks lie for any given manager. Despite significant media attention to some of these areas, they keep popping up in operational reviews. Please note these areas are not presented in any particular order.

1. Complacency—
Trivializing and Disregarding Risks

Risk," February 2003, p. 2. The definition as given here originally appeared in "Working Paper on the Regulatory Treatment of Operational Risk," September 2001, p. 8. Stone House Consulting accepts the exclusion of reputational risk from the definition but postulates that internal operational risk *entails* reputational risk. We maintain that the reputational consequences arising from "inadequate or failed internal processes, people and systems" should be captured in a comprehensive measure of operational risk. For instance, the firm might model the loss of investment management fees as assets are withdrawn.

2. The Blind Leading the Blind—
   Overextended and Underqualified Managers

3. Novices, Apprentices and Soloists—
   Inadequate Training or Cross-Training

4. Dropped Batons—
   Hand-Offs

5. Naïve Reliance on Technology—
   The Downside of Automation

6. Playbooks—
   Workflow Documentation

7. Amalgamated Assignments—
   Improper Segregation of Duties

8. Reconciliation Gaps—
   A False Sense of Security

9. Reading the Fine Print—
   Know Thy Legal Entities

10. Poor Planning and Slow Response Times—
    Changes in the Firm, the Marketplace and the Regulatory Environment

We remarked that operational risk may be seen as "risk without reward." In this view, there is no upside for the firm, and operations managers are compensated on the pinball model: if they do very well, they get to play again. We'd like to suggest another perspective. Operational excellence, which starts with risk management, can create value by reducing costs, increasing client satisfaction and maintaining sound business relationships with trading partners. We hope you will enjoy reading these chapters and that you find them to be both thought-provoking and practical.

OPERATIONAL RISK ONE
COMPLACENCY
Trivializing and Disregarding Risks

WE have all heard the term "culture of compliance" and most of us know that it refers to an organizational ethos of playing by the rules. But we all know those people—and organizations—that just don't get it.

We find the same situation in the domain of operational risk. Some firms and some managers just don't worry about it. "So far, so good. We have policies in place; we've always had them. Everything is under control. In fact, we've had some near misses that demonstrate we're on top of it. Whoa, look at the time, I'm late for a meeting!"

To some extent we are all guilty of complacency. The seat belts that remain unbuckled because we're only driving around the corner. The cell phones and PDAs that aren't password-protected because it's annoying. The cups of coffee that are precariously close to the edges of our cluttered desks because we're focused on the task at hand.

It is one thing to take a risk with personal safety and personal property (although some clients justifiably want to be assured their managers are physically and financially healthy). But without question investment management firms must take care to identify, mitigate and monitor the risks that could jeopardize client assets and the health of the organization itself.

Complacent organizations and managers will fall into a passive approach toward operational risk rather than adopting a proactive one. They will react to headline risks (e.g., Madoff or 9/11) rather than carefully and seriously thinking about what could go wrong. Evidence of this laid-back attitude can be found in flawed business continuity plans (is any consideration given to the potential loss of staff in a worst-case scenario?), poor recordkeeping (is there a chronic backlog of documents to be scanned?) and deficient insurance coverage (are there adequate policies in force for errors and omissions as well as general liability and directors and officers?).

Staffing is a key area in which complacency is unaffordable. Hiring inexperienced or under-qualified staff—especially in the current market environment when so many good people are available—introduces significant operational risk to an organization, and neglecting to train new employees compounds the error. (We'll have more to say about staffing and training later in this book.) In the same vein, many firms fail to appreciate the complexity of the products they offer or the financial instruments they trade. For example, the skills and systems required to support the management of fixed-income securities generally are more advanced than those needed for a firm that focuses exclusively on equity instruments. Likewise, investing outside one's own country requires substantially more data elements and operational effort. Emerging markets or derivatives can introduce even more variables. Proactive investment managers will recognize the importance of aligning staff skills with operational complexity and hire or train appropriately.

Disregarding the inputs from middle- and back-office staff is another risk commonly associated with complacency (not to mention its first cousin, arrogance). Aside from their ability to suggest ways to reduce the probability of errors within their own areas, these staff members often see risks that originate elsewhere in the organization. For instance, they may be on the receiving end of consistently incorrect or belated trade entries by a particular trader, or they may see sales and marketing teams changing presentation materials after a compliance review is completed. Use of a new counterparty or an unfamiliar security type without a heads-up to operations and IT can often result in significantly increased risk of failed trades that could have been avoided without any additional expense to the firm.

On the other hand, a good sign of an investment manager with a proactive attitude toward operational risk is when senior management listens to the feedback offered by its support teams and takes action to resolve any critical issues those teams may raise. All investment management firms should maintain *and review* error logs that capture both errors and near misses—red flags whose instructional value must not be squandered. Many firms have established a formal new product committee that includes not only investment and sales/marketing staff, but also compliance, operations and IT.

> Think about whether you reward, punish or ignore news of a risk

The presence or absence of some sort of electronic document management capability also indicates whether a firm has a passive or active approach toward operational risk. Are investment management agreements, guidelines and objectives, client correspondence and other contracts scanned and backed up? Or are they sitting in locked file cabinets that could be rendered useless if there are plumbing issues on the floor above[1] or the firm is forced to relocate to its disaster recovery site? In these days of inexpensive document scanners and cloud computing, even the smallest investment man-

---

[1] On 16 September 2010, one month after we originally wrote this sentence, a water pipe burst on the JPMorgan trading floor at 10 Aldermanbury, London.

agers can afford to ensure these critical documents are effectively backed up. (Note: Any readers who are still unconcerned should read the SEC's July 2000 response to Jennison Associates' request for a no-action letter.[2] In a warehouse fire, Jennison lost records that supported the firm's performance track record.)

A final aspect of complacency we often see is typically confused with trust. Many investment managers simply trust the people on their teams to get the job done and get it done right. "I hire good people," they say, "and then get out of their way." While seemingly laudable, such blind trust actually is a disservice to team members, as those who have reported to absentee managers can attest. Failing to check whether an account was reconciled properly, performance-based fees were calculated correctly or a compliance rule was interpreted and coded rightly leaves all the responsibility for accuracy on the staff member performing the work. It is generally better to have someone else check your work from time to time. (Think how easy it is to miss your own spelling mistakes and grammatical lapses.) In addition, when it comes to issues like fraud and embezzlement, we all appreciate working under procedures that ensure we cannot be placed under a cloud of suspicion. Rather than displaying a lack of trust, proper checks and balances demonstrate a manager's commitment to risk management on behalf of both clients and staff.

So take a minute. Consider what could "bite" your firm. Ask your staff the same question. Think about whether you reward, punish or ignore news of a risk. And then work on some ways to keep these potential problems from ever happening. Who knows? It could be simple. Like moving your coffee cup.

---

[2] sec.gov/divisions/investment/noaction/2000/jennison070600.pdf

OPERATIONAL RISK TWO
THE BLIND LEADING THE BLIND
Overextended and Underqualified Managers

SUPERVISION is second on our list of common areas of operational risk because we see breakdowns so often and in so many different forms. As those who have supervised staff know all too well, it is one thing to manage what we do and something entirely different to direct the decisions and activities of others. The larger the firm, the more difficult the task. And organizations that have outsourced critical support services to specialists—often in an endeavor to reduce operational risk—frequently discover that managing the process is more effortful and expensive than anticipated.

Having been assigned responsibility for activities with which they are unfamiliar, many mid-level and senior managers simply are not up to the task of supervising operational functions. This is not merely a problem in small firms that cannot yet afford to hire specialists in such domains as human resources, accounting, operations and systems. At some point in the evolution of larger organizations, too, managers are no longer hands-on supervisors with the time and knowledge to perform any job on their team; instead, they become executives who must rely on the experience and expertise of their direct reports. Some well-established companies offer a management-training program in which high-potential recruits (many with MBAs or other professional credentials) are rotated around the organization to establish a network and learn about the workings of various areas. Most military organizations adopt a similar approach over time for officers with a bright future.

Yet within most buy-side firms, the chief executive officer typically comes from the investment or distribution side of the organization. To date, operations, compliance and technology have not been seen as incubators for the CEO's position. In addition, few investment management firms have a management-training program. As a result, few buy-side leaders have a solid understanding of the workings of the middle and back office, much less a firm grasp of the details involved in identifying and managing operational risk.[1] This inexperience leaves many senior executives at a loss when evaluating the advice provided by their direct reports or even when assessing how well these teams perform. They have to fall back upon their instincts at the risk of mistaking the most persuasive for the most knowledgeable. Much of the indifference toward operations, IT and compliance that pervades the buy-side today stems from ignorance of the complexity inherent in those areas. If this statement seems unduly harsh, we invite you to trade war stories with your colleagues over the beverage of your choice at the end of a long, hard day. We certainly have a few of our own.

Failure to appreciate operational complexity often results in managers delegating responsibility to others who may also be unqualified for the task assigned. One common example of this situa-

---

[1] We are not the first consulting firm serving the investment management industry to make this observation. See Casey, Quirk & Acito's insightful remarks on business management at first- and second-generation firms in their seminal 2003 white paper, "Success in Investment Management: Three Years Later." In our view, however, the expectation of better business management skills and practices among "complete firms" of the next generation remains largely unfulfilled.

tion is when CEOs assign all responsibility for operational risk to an understaffed compliance team composed entirely of attorneys and paralegals. To suggest that a law degree or a regulatory background qualifies someone to identify and mitigate technological or operational risk is as misguided as calling upon an IT or operations expert to prepare the offering documents for a fund. And it raises a question of corporate governance: Who oversees compliance?

Inexperience with operations and IT can lead to injudicious decisions when CEOs attempt to outsource their risk along with their operations. There are many well-founded reasons to outsource, but without careful management of the process firms may actually increase their operational risk profile rather than reducing it. Tony Hayward, erstwhile CEO of BP, illustrated this point with unconscious irony in May 2010 when he said, "This was not our drilling rig, it was not our equipment, it was not our people, our systems or our processes....We are taking our responsibility to deal with it very, very seriously."[2]

> Few buy-side leaders have a solid understanding of the workings of the middle and back office

It is a philosophical commonplace that the first step toward wisdom is to stop thinking we know what we don't. Senior managers who endorse the idea of lifelong learning might welcome an overview of the firm's operations, including graphical representations of the systems architecture and various workflows. They might, for example, be fascinated to discover how a new account is opened, or what happens after a portfolio manager says "buy this" or "sell that." The goal is not to make operational experts of senior managers whose home discipline is investing or marketing; it is merely to help them ask the right questions about the other risks to which the firm and its stakeholders are exposed. In addition, external assessments such as mock regulatory examinations, peer benchmarking and operational due diligence reviews, conducted under strict nondisclosure agree-

---

[2] BBC News interview 5 May 2010.

ments, may not only identify improvement opportunities but also indicate whether CEOs should continue to rely upon their direct reports. Some firms may decide to create or strengthen internal audit departments for recurrent monitoring.[3]

Key service providers such as accountants, custodians, prime brokers, fund administrators and software vendors also introduce operational risk, but few investment management firms—even those that have, themselves, been placed under the microscope by prospective clients—seem to put concerted effort into the due diligence they perform. Effective risk management in this domain calls for more than simply hiring a big name and/or moving to a multi-prime service model. We would suggest issuing RFPs, obtaining financial statements (nobody can interpret them better than security analysts), performing annual on-site visits and reading the fine print. We will return to the fine print in a forthcoming chapter (it is Operational Risk Nine).

During the 2007-2009 downturn many buy-side firms reduced staff, and in some cases support teams bore the brunt of those cutbacks. However, the number of securities transactions did not decline—on the contrary, the volume of trades on the New York Stock Exchange rose throughout the crisis[4]—and today we often see firms stretched to the limit. Some managers have such a wide span of managerial responsibility that it is impossible to keep track of all their direct reports' activities.

> **The first step toward wisdom is to stop thinking we know what we don't**

Others have been placed in the dual role of manager and individual contributor. As the job market improves, firms who treated their staff poorly will find themselves with too few to get the job done;

---

[3] In our opinion, it is more effective to have internal auditors who also understand enterprise risk management in the financial services industry than to employ ERM specialists without audit experience. The ideal, unfortunately far from the norm, is to have audit and ERM experience within investment management.

[4] NYSE Group Share and Dollar Volume in NYSE Listed, 2009.

indeed, the managers themselves may leave. In a well-intentioned effort to promote from within, some firms might create an environment where team leaders are in over their heads.

External operational reviews can assist with determining whether there are organizational risks within a firm. In any case, it is good practice to update job descriptions and implement succession planning for all key positions. (Please note that a very junior position can still be vital.) Hiring qualified staff at all levels of an organization can help ensure succession plans are realistic. Training and cross-training preserve institutional history and knowledge. Workflow documentation memorializes processes, procedures and accountabilities and facilitates effective training. (We will address potential issues with workflow documentation in the forthcoming chapter, Operational Risk Six: Playbooks.) For those investment managers who want to grow their organizations without hiring back the number of employees it was so painful to lay off, a long-term plan for improved automation may offer a solution. We'll have more to say about automation in another chapter (Operational Risk Five: Naïve Reliance on Technology).

No discussion of operational risk would be complete without a mention of rogue activity. Yet not all rogues are cheats, nor do all seek only to enrich themselves. Many want to do a good job but have found a shortcut or had to triage their functions because they are overstretched. (Often they intend to catch up and, for instance, review all those past reconciliations at some unspecified future time.) A senior staff member ignoring policies and procedures is another common type of rogue activity, especially in smaller firms. Maintaining an operational risk log and requiring those involved in an event or near miss to document and present the issue may help educate violators or, at a minimum, shame them into compliance. In some instances, firms simply need to enforce policies that already exist; where there are chronic offenses, however, new enforcement policies may need to be established (such as imposing fines or withholding pay until those personal trading forms have been filed).

We'll stop here. We've postponed cross-training on our payroll system long enough!

OPERATIONAL RISK THREE
NOVICES, APPRENTICES AND SOLOISTS
Inadequate Training or Cross-Training

WE have previously mentioned training and cross-training several times as a key tool for mitigating operational risk. But the lack of adequate training and cross-training within operational departments is so widespread that it also stands on its own as third on our list of risk areas.

Much of the challenge comes from poor organizational design. Many firms have built highly specialized operational teams to handle a specific asset class, investment strategy, client or fund. For example, we often see firms that have assembled small groups to focus on high-yield fixed income, OTC derivatives or bank debt. In many organizations there are dedicated teams for each large fund. The appeal of such an approach is obvious: management can put their best people in a particularly challenging area, clients like to hear that a team was dedicated to their account or fund and staff are less distracted by other demands on their time. Indeed, many investment managers create these specialized teams in an effort to lower their operational risk profiles.

Unfortunately, however, all too often this myopic approach generates more risk rather than less. A small, specialized team's intellectual capital and institutional knowledge may be severely depleted by the loss of a single member. Such losses may be short-term in nature (such as a vacation), of moderate duration (such as maternity leave) or permanent (perhaps a promotion). Aside from the duration of this brain drain, one of the key risks is the abruptness with which it can occur. Illnesses, family emergencies and resignations typically involve little or no notice and leave organizations scrambling to cope.

Murphy's Law frequently comes into play in these scenarios because their timing often couldn't be worse. Whether the family emergency happens during month-end processing or the resignation occurs when other key staff are on holiday, in many instances firms suffer from a double-whammy—a loss of key knowledge during a period of high volume and/or skeletal staffing. It is also taxing to lose good people when a product launch or a system conversion is imminent.

Our concerns on this front are elevated in the current market environment. Throughout our industry, firms reduced middle- and back-office staffing during the recent market crisis and now have little room for any additional loss of people. As the job market continues to improve, we foresee a rise in staff turnover—particularly at those firms who did not treat their staff well during the downturn. Investment managers with low morale may see their most employable people jump ship the moment the opportunity arises.

The specialized-team approach also fosters isolation and frequently results in an unnecessarily high number of workflows. Instead of minimally customizing a master set of workflows, each team develops its own processes and procedures. We will delve into this issue more thoroughly in our upcoming chapter on workflows (Operational Risk #6: Playbooks), but it should be kept in mind when considering how to organize support teams.

Business continuity planning is another reason we have heightened concerns at present around training and cross-training. If we were to face another catastrophic terrorist attack, a SARS or swine-flu scenario, an earthquake, a hurricane or a major snowstorm, even firms who have not suffered a loss of staff might find themselves short-handed because their teams were unwilling or unable to come to the office.

We touched on the lack of training for managers in our previous chapter, Operational Risk Two: The Blind Leading the Blind. We find much the same situation at lower organizational levels where the work actually gets done. When we interview junior staff in the course of an operational review, we often find they are unable to explain their job in the context of their overall department. Indeed, many cannot articulate what their firm actually *does*. Without seeing how their individual role fits into the larger organization, staff cannot appreciate the urgency of information, the importance of accuracy or how much minor improvements would benefit their colleagues and boost productivity. For example, every reconciliation clerk should understand the potential impact a position break could have on the investment team and the trading desk. Yet shockingly, all too often one side of the organization has no idea what happens on the other side. How many traders understand the downstream impacts—and costs—of an erroneous trade ticket?

> Relationships belong to the firm, not the relationship manager

Employees with a narrow view of their own workplace are unlikely to understand how other organizations tackle the same problems your company faces. It is specious to think one firm or one department has found the best approach without first considering solutions that other organizations have devised. This is a particular hazard for firms that have enjoyed minimal staff turnover through the years but whose staff do not regularly attend conferences and network with their peers in the industry. In such cases, many organizations develop processes and procedures that might once have been efficient but have not kept pace with industry practice and technological change. Firms that encourage lifelong learning may have a lasting competitive advantage because their staff are engaged and their solutions are up-to-date.

The phrase "on-the-job training" (OJT) may mask the absence of any coherent training. However, poorly trained novices are not the only pertinent source of operational risk. Well-trained soloists can also impede or sabotage salubrious attempts to mitigate key-person risk through cross-training. These individuals manage to become the only person in the firm who can perform a specific function or the sole guardian of a specific client relationship.

Generally, the presence of a soloist is a warning sign. As we have pointed out before, key-man risk is not limited to senior staff and often is found in the most low-ranking, mundane positions within an organization.[1] For example, many organizations have soloists performing functions that no one else wants to learn. Payroll processing or security master maintenance can be tedious.

Team size, then, is not the only indicator of a cross-training issue. Many large sales or client service teams provide a safe haven for soloists who actively balk at allowing others to service key relationships they have nurtured for years. Relationships belong to the firm, not the relationship manager. Yet many RMs seem to have lost track of this key point. They are the ones who feel that their contacts are just that—*their* contacts—and never get around to updating the client relationship management (CRM) system. And their supervisors don't correct them for fear of rocking the boat.

Effective training can be obtained in a variety of ways. There is not yet a professional credentialing program in investment operations, but the Certificate in Investment Performance Measurement (CIPM®) offered by CFA Institute ensures that performance practitioners have the requisite skills in their specialized field. Many classes and short courses, both live and online, are available across

---

[1] In some cases, training and cross-training may not be an issue, but only one person has sufficient system access rights to perform a particular function. The key-person risk remains.

a wide range of topics.[2] Customized onsite training is also an option. Attending webinars, industry conferences and networking events is a great approach for many, particularly those who are knowledgeable in their jobs but would benefit from more exposure to other organizations.

A series of internal "lunch-and-learn" sessions is an effective approach to cross-training, and more often than not the participants also discover opportunities for operational improvements. Job rotation, job shadowing and job swaps are also great ways to ensure cross-training takes place, especially if they are accompanied by presentations on the systems architecture and workflows. In addition, the individual who leads a training session stands to benefit from the experience.

Identifying training and cross-training challenges generally is not difficult. Start by looking at your organization chart to identify small teams. (We recommend that teams never be smaller than three fully cross-trained people.) Ensure all clients have primary and back-up relationship managers and that both individuals have regular contact with each client assigned to them. Quiz staff on what they should have read in the firm's compliance manual or code of ethics. Review system access capabilities. Spot-check CRM updates. Ask people to describe what they do—*and really listen to their answers*.

Test your cross-training results by implementing a largely bygone banking practice: the mandatory two-week vacation without any access to the office or systems. Your staff and their significant others will thank you for it!

---

[2] Stone House Consulting is one of many training resources for the investment industry. Please visit http://www.stonehouseconsulting.com/Events/Events.html for information about upcoming classes, webinars and presentations.

OPERATIONAL RISK FOUR
DROPPED BATONS
Hand-offs

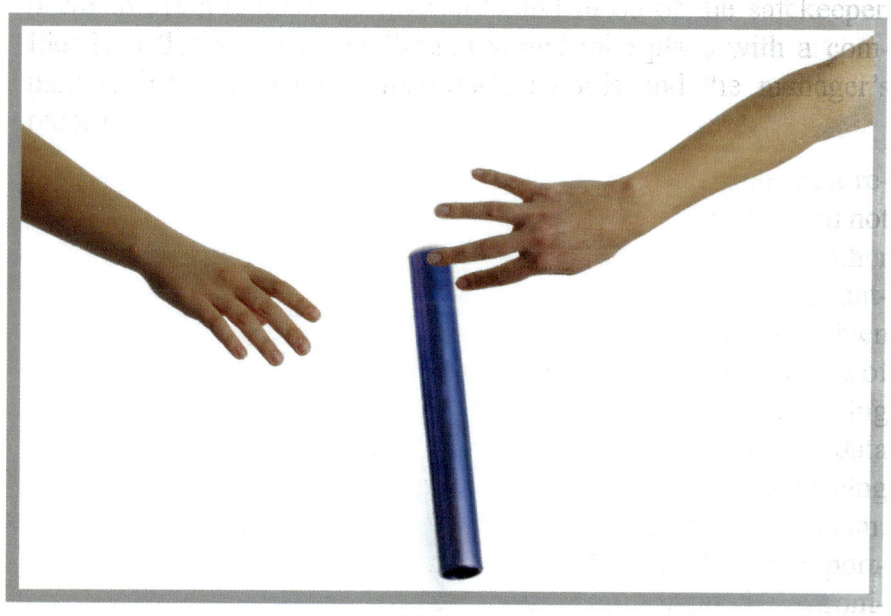

COMPETITIVE runners know that in a 400-meter relay significant time can be lost passing the baton from one sprinter to another if someone fumbles or, worse still, drops the baton. Individual runners may excel but the team still loses the race. Traditional and alternative investment managers face similar risks when passing information between people, departments, organizations and systems involved in complex series of sequential activities. Hand-offs are fraught with communication and timing challenges; that's why superior relay teams practice their baton-handling techniques and well-managed operational units are particularly attentive to interchanges of any sort.

A great way to think about hand-offs—and how to manage them—is to revisit the dark days of paper tickets. In fact, a handful of firms are still using this time-honored method, and it is an approach that works adequately with limited volumes.[1] But tickets can get lost because someone mislaid them, a data entry clerk forgot to input them or they simply fell behind a file cabinet.

Eventually best-practice organizations would count the number of tickets written and the number of trades entered to the firm's investment accounting system, comparing the two totals at the end of the day. If 218 tickets had been written and only 217 had been entered to the system, then one was missing and a search was initiated. This approach didn't completely address the problem (if another trade had been entered twice, then the counts would appear to be correct), but it did help to eliminate some of the trouble. Marking tickets that were entered to the system helped address duplicate trade entry, and purchasing wire baskets to hold tickets eliminated at least some of the lost-behind-the-file-cabinet issues.

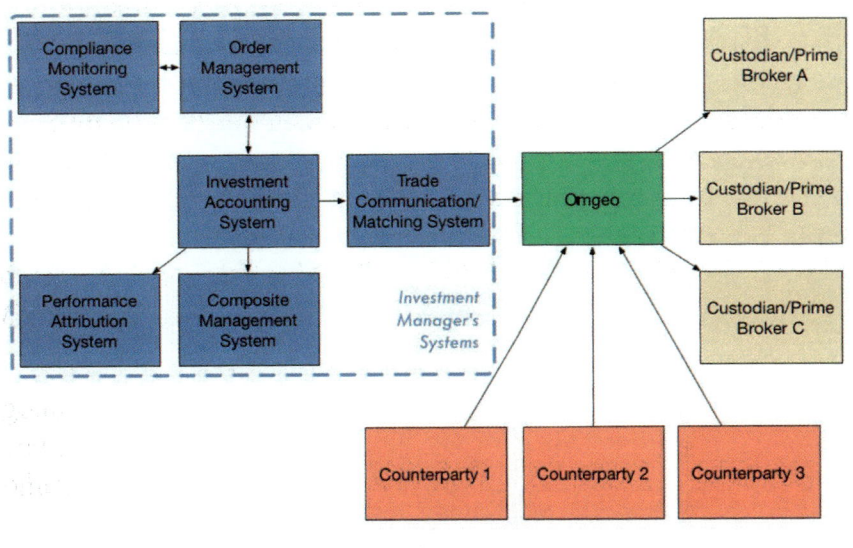

Exhibit 1 – Sample Systems Diagram

These days—we'll resist the temptation to say "nowadays"—we have less paper, fewer wire baskets and more automation. Of course, we also have far higher transactional volumes and often

---

[1] We refer managers who are using paper tickets to our article, "Critical Recordkeeping: Trade Tickets and Order Memoranda," available at articles.stonehouseconsulting.com.

more moving parts within the firm as well as with trading partners, custodians, prime brokers, administrators, exchanges and settlement facilities. The concepts, however, remain the same.

We like to start looking for hand-offs using two simple but powerful tools. The first is a good system diagram (see Exhibit 1) that should identify every application in use and the interfaces between applications. The second is workflow diagramming. In particular, we like to use swim-lane diagrams (see Exhibit 2) to determine where hand-offs occur.

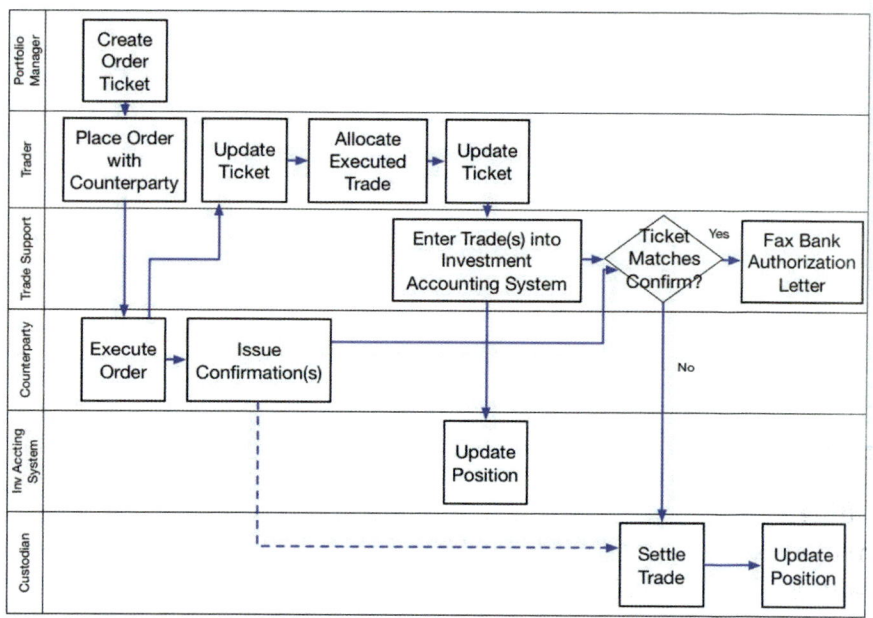

Exhibit 2 – Sample Swimlane Diagram

We will come back to interface issues in our next chapter (Operational Risk Five: Naïve Reliance on Technology), but for now suffice it to say that hand-offs between two systems are highly suspect as potential trouble spots. Often they were not planned well at the outset (e.g., built for equities but not fixed income because "we'll never need that"). They may also be poorly written, inadequately documented (or not documented at all), unsupported by either system vendor, and difficult to maintain when one system or the other gets upgraded. All too often no one has looked at them for a long time, and no one who is still in the firm's employ knows exactly how they function.

Good workflow diagrams include systems, giving each its own swim lane, so that interactions between people and systems can be captured (again, think of entering data from paper tickets). These diagrams also capture hand-offs between teams or departments, between one firm and another (such as receiving execution details from a counterparty and sending back trade allocation information) and between the investment manager and its clients (such as client reports or subscription and redemption activity).

Once an exchange has been captured, we consider how often the hand-off occurs, the information transferred, the timing around the hand-off and the sorts of things that can go wrong with it. We find it helpful to look at available metrics, procedural documentation, data requirements and error logs to evaluate the scope, nature and potential impact of operational mishaps. Returning to our example, a ticket could be lost or entered twice. It might be illegible or contain bad information in one or more fields. It might also be submitted late, for instance, after the data entry team has gone home for the night. In addition, it is possible the security—or the counterparty, the currency or even the portfolio—has not been set up yet, or set up correctly, in the investment accounting system.

> **Hand-offs are fraught with communication and timing challenges**

Armed with a complete inventory of what can go wrong, we can address the likelihood of each and the damage or trouble a problem might cause. We can also begin to build workflows, processes and escalation protocols to mitigate the risks. For example, if a security or currency has not been set up, a simple fix for some firms might be to set the missing item up on the spot. For other organizations, however, the solution may not be so straightforward. For example, if trade entry clerks are not authorized or trained in new security or counterparty set-up, a further hand-off takes place between trade entry and the security/counterparty maintenance group. Extending the example of the late trade ticket, perhaps someone from the trade entry team was still in the office, working late, but no one is around to set up the security. This new hand-off needs its own examination of risks and how to mitigate them.

Most of our suggestions for mitigating these issues will be covered in other chapters. But we do encourage careful examination of hand-offs, establishing metrics around each wherever possible and creating processes that check back to ensure a hand-off was successfully completed. Those firms with outsourced investment operations should examine hand-offs to and from their outsourcing provider. (Providers—this applies to your organizations as well!) Each hand-off should be covered by a service-level agreement (SLA) with deadlines, quality expectations and metrics to evaluate the performance of both the provider *and* the investment manager.

When looking at hand-offs, please do not forget to consider clients. Even the most sophisticated institutional clients sometimes fail to notify managers of contributions or withdrawals in separate accounts. Such failures create needless reconciliation work for harried operations staff and can lead to distorted or misattributed returns. In our experience, portfolio managers are more likely to forgive the client than the operations group when their performance is dinged because the client neglected to inform the firm of a cash flow.

Perhaps clients with outstanding invoices have deposited funds to our account without letting us know. We'd better go check!

OPERATIONAL RISK FIVE

NAÏVE RELIANCE ON TECHNOLOGY
The Downside of Automation

SOME knowledgeable analysts contend that banks' and investment managers' misplaced trust in automated market risk models such as value-at-risk (VAR) contributed to the financial crisis of 2007–2008.[1] Whether the models misestimated the riskiness of leveraged positions or the users misinterpreted the models' output, senior managers with oversight responsibility may have convinced themselves that they fully understood their firm's exposures—that is to say, the vulnerability of their clients, shareholders, and employees—to unlikely events, and that the risks were tolerable.

---

[1] Bruce J. Feibel, "VARred and Feathered: Value at Risk and the Global Financial Crisis," CFA Institute Investment Performance Measurement Newsletter, June 2010.

The global economy is still in recovery.

As we have previously observed, operational and IT staff were well-represented among the financial services employees displaced as the crisis unfolded. Ironically, however, naïve reliance upon technology is also a meaningful source of investment managers' operational risk. We'll identify major areas of concern in this chapter.

But let's be clear from the start: automation is frequently the best approach to mitigating operational risk. Computers are terrific. Properly selected, programmed and managed, they can perform repetitive tasks without growing bored or inattentive. They tend to perform tasks faster than people do; consider high-volume trading systems' ability to enter transactions in fractions of a second.[2] Computers are willing to work 24/7, and you never find that they have run downstairs for a cup of coffee or outside for a cigarette.

> Computers also have the capacity to spew out mistakes at superhuman speed

Yet computers also have the capacity to spew out mistakes at superhuman speed. Moreover, unlike the qualified, well-trained and cross-trained operational staff we've called for in this book, computers are fundamentally obtuse. They will do only what we tell them to do, and then, like a surly adolescent, they will do *exactly* what we say. They won't demonstrate initiative; for example, computers will not perform a reasonability check unless we specifically instruct them to do so and define "reasonable" in unambiguous, syntactically correct terms. In June 2010, an international bank's algorithmic trading system acted on bad pricing inputs by placing 7,468 orders to sell Nikkei 225 futures contracts on the Osaka Stock Exchange. The total value was more than $182 billion. Any trader would have questioned the size of the transaction, but the system's

---

[2] The post-mortem regulatory studies are still in progress, but the speed of high-volume trading systems indubitably contributed to the flash crash of 6 May 2010.

developers hadn't taught the system to make such evaluations, and approximately $546 million of the orders were executed before the error was caught. Ultimately the bank was reprimanded by the exchange, shut down the proprietary trading unit in question and received a great deal of unfavorable publicity.

In the domain of investment operations, trouble may stem from automating activities that people never knew or have forgotten how to do manually. Thanks to the widespread availability of calculators, many of us have to stop and think when called upon to compute a tip at a restaurant. It is no wonder that the finer points of accrued interest calculations may be lost on a younger generation that never had to perform such computations by hand. Can we expect them to determine whether a fixed-income system is applying the correct day-count convention to US corporate bonds (generally 30/360) as opposed to US Treasury bonds (actual/actual)?

In our estimation, proper automation requires a thorough knowledge of performing the activity manually. Without such a fundamental understanding, it is impossible to consider the necessary steps in a process—as well as those that might *not* be necessary in an automated environment—and to make certain that vital functions, steps with consequences, are not skipped. Likewise, it is impossible to test a new system or feature thoroughly without considering the manual activities the system or feature will replace. Staff who know how something is done also know how mistakes are made—and they know when correct results are determined by the application.

Failure to see systems in their operational context is a related source of trouble. Investment managers have invested significant time and money to implement pre-trade compliance systems intended to flag or block transactions which, if executed, would result in breaching an account's investment guidelines. But we see these same firms enable traders to set up skeleton securities on the fly. If the firm were purchasing Exxon for the first time, the trader could set up a common stock skeleton security with the security name, ticker and currency so that trading can proceed apace. Other details, such as Exxon's primary exchange, indicated annual dividend or sector and industry classifications, will be filled in later by someone else. While this procedure certainly accelerates the trading process, the investment management firm has impaired its state-of-the-art pre-trade compliance system. How can the system evaluate the percentage held in energy stocks if it does not know that Exxon should be classified within energy?

Poorly designed or implemented technology solutions can be found throughout an investment management firm. In some situations, a manager is using a system that was not built for the type of portfolios or instruments the firm manages. For instance, an investment manager may be trying to support a handful of multi-currency client portfolios using a single-currency investment accounting system, or trading fixed-income securities on a system originally designed only to handle equities. In other cases, the manager may be relying on Excel® spreadsheets or an Access® database in lieu of an application that has been tested and locked down to protect against *ad hoc* changes.

As indicated in our previous chapter, Operational Risk Four: Dropped Batons, interfaces between two systems are particularly suspect. This is especially true if they were originally built in a phased implementation process to accommodate a subset of the information that could be transferred between them.[3] Too often, the early project phases were poorly documented and subsequent phases are delayed, leaving IT and operations departments unsure how an interface will perform when confronted with a new set of inputs. We know the interface works with common stocks; will it cope with preferreds?

In an earlier chapter, Operational Risk Three: Novices, Apprentices and Soloists, we alluded to systems access capabilities. Many well-designed buy-side applications allow an investment manager to control access at the function level. For example, traders could be authorized to enter trades but prohibited from setting up securities, and portfolio managers might be able to view information and run reports but not to change any data. Some firms neglect to

---

[3] For example, the investment manager might implement the system initially to support equities only, delaying the support of fixed-income and derivatives instruments for later phases of the project.

implement these built-in system controls. Other organizations establish the controls but fail to update them as workflows are altered, systems capabilities are upgraded and people change jobs. Jérôme Kerviel's fraud at Société Générale was facilitated, in part, by a failure to keep systems access privileges up-to-date.

Improper or incomplete audit trails are a key risk area with some older vendor systems as well as many newer, less robust applications. Needless to say, it is pandemic with electronic spreadsheets and relational databases created without corporate oversight by business units that cannot wait for IT resources to become available. However, it may prove important to know who changed a price or canceled a trade or set up a security, on what date, and at what time of day. A reliable audit trail will not only help during regulatory exams but also assist in unwinding errors, designing process controls and identifying additional training needs.

> **Failure to keep software up-to-date is perilous**

In the introduction to this book, we promised not only to describe operational risks but also to offer guidance on mitigating them. Readers may begin to notice certain themes in our advice since some of the tools we recommend can be used to address different risk areas.

Systems diagrams and workflow diagramming facilitate identifying key interfaces and establishing and maintaining system access rights. Properly executed, these diagrams will also identify all systems in use, including spreadsheets and proprietary databases, so that potential audit trail issues can be brought to light and addressed.

However costly and time-consuming it may be, maintaining the firm's systems infrastructure is a process that should not be overlooked or casually postponed. Investment managers may engage teams of consultants to assist with a new system implementation but fail to ensure the firm remains adequately and appropriately staffed to install and test new system releases (as well as the workflow and interface modifications and changes to business continuity plans they may entail). Failure to keep software up-to-date is perilous:

new releases may contain critical bug fixes and vendor contracts often limit support to recent releases. In their haste to keep from falling too far behind, some managers curtail their testing process for software releases or skip the testing altogether, taking on risks that would make their clients shudder.

The mention of consultants brings us to an important point. Our industry (that is, the investment management consulting industry) can help dramatically with mitigating operational risk, particularly through well-directed operational reviews, system or outsourcing vendor evaluation and selection processes and implementation projects. But consultants can also contribute to operational risk. Here are a few tips for managing them effectively.

Ascertain that consultants know the business of investment management, not just financial services in general. (We do things differently on the buy side.) For an evaluation/selection project, ensure that any consultant under consideration is independent or has fully disclosed any compensation arrangements with vendors. In an implementation project, the vendor's specialists provide knowledge of the most up-to-date releases and bug fixes as well as priority access to the vendor's support team in the event an issue arises. Remember, however, that vendor-supplied implementation consultants may not have experience working within a buy-side firm and consequently may be unaware of best-practice workflows or the upstream and downstream impacts of key activities or errors. On a large-scale system or outsourcing implementation, it is advisable to engage specialized consultants as well as the vendor consultants to ensure your firm's priorities and objectives are kept in sharp focus. And confirm that consultants have a plan for transferring their knowledge to your staff during the project. Otherwise you may be working with them forever.

While we are on the topic of technology and people, we should briefly mention the relationship between operations and IT. Some years ago, we saw the IT departments in many investment management firms dictate the systems that would be used to support operations. More recently the pendulum has swung back in favor of operations calling the shots. We believe strongly that IT and operations staff must work hand-in-glove to create an effective infrastructure. IT needs to support operations rather than mandate solutions. At the same time, operations must be sensitive to IT's perspective on the costs and requirements of some potential solutions. Only through a well-aligned and cooperative relationship between these two key areas will the firm build and maintain an effective operational risk environment.

Evidently we added a modest tip for unexceptional service to a dinner bill that already included an 18% service charge. A generous, compound gratuity. No wonder the wait staff seemed so pleased.

OPERATIONAL RISK SIX
PLAYBOOKS
Workflow Documentation

WE have frequently had occasion to mention workflow diagramming and documentation in these chapters. Documenting processes and procedures is such a fundamental and obvious requirement for effective operations management that our belaboring it again may seem unwarranted. Nonetheless, inexistent, obsolete or incomplete documentation is implicated in so many operational snafus that we would be remiss if we did not single it out as an area of risk in its own right. Even if you are among the managers whose documentation is useful, comprehensive, up-to-date and readily accessible in an emergency, you may find the few minutes it takes to read this chapter time well spent. If, on the other hand, the state of your documentation is worrisome, you may wish not only to read on but also to use this chapter as the basis of dialogue within your firm or department. You have work to do! Let's get started.

At the extreme, some groups (especially but not exclusively at emerging firms) simply do not have any formal workflows at all. Instead, the team is managed on the whack-a-mole model, with predictable consequences for the quality of work-life. When the entire firm lacks a playbook, the chaotic result often resembles an undisciplined team of six-year-olds playing a game of soccer in which the entire team—offensive and defensive players alike—race after the ball at all times. (Some parents call this "magnet ball.") Without workflows, it is impossible to ensure operational controls are in place, staff are performing all critical tasks and all systems in use, especially mission-critical spreadsheets, have been identified. The total absence of workflow diagrams or documentation could and should signal an abrupt end to any operational due diligence review meeting.

Out-of-date workflows are another common challenge for investment managers. Reorganizations, systems implementations, product launches, new reporting requirements, changes to system access levels and new instrument types are all compelling reasons for updating workflows. Even managers at well-established, relatively stable firms where nothing significant appears to have changed should take a fresh look at their workflows at least annually.

> Good workflows also come in handy when training new employees

We have written elsewhere about overcoming the impediments to creating and maintaining useful documentation—lack of time, lack of staff motivation and lack of expertise.[1] Usefulness, however, is an elusive quality. Overly vague documentation is unhelpful in a crisis, while excessively detailed documentation generally has such a short shelf life that the material loses value before it is critically needed. Perfectionism is an occupational hazard for disciplined, analytical minds, but effective operations managers have to be results-oriented. In our experience step-by-step documentation that goes

---

[1] "Mitigating Lottery Risk," *Performance Measurement and Client Reporting Review*, Vol. 3.1, Autumn 2010. Reprinted below by permission of Osney Media.

to the point of including screen shots and keystrokes is rarely worth the considerable effort and expense it entails. The manager and the firm may be better served by supplementing reasonably informative documentation with extensive cross-training. The appropriate level of documentation is, however, a matter of individual judgment, taking into account the firm's and the department's overall preparedness for disaster recovery.

Good workflows also come in handy when training new employees. Onboarding new staff is often challenging, and new employees can find themselves with nothing to do while team members deal with meetings, phone calls or emails. Reviewing workflows is a perfect activity during those idle periods, and it ensures new staff learn from the start the right way to do their jobs. Miscommunication is less likely to occur. There is another benefit: new employees' feedback can help you gauge the clarity and effectiveness of the documentation.

In our chapter on training and cross-training, Operational Risk Three: Novices, Apprentices and Soloists, we reviewed the risks that can arise when firms develop small, specialized teams by product, instrument type, investment strategy or client. Often these small teams will all start with a single set of workflows used across all similar teams in the organization. Over time, however, each team will customize their processes and procedures, perhaps without documenting these refinements. The outcome can be a firm with multiple sets of workflows for the same basic function, such as trade settlement or reconciliation. When we encounter these situations and question the result, teams often protest, "We're different!"

Consider the workflows for pouring and serving coffee. We could have four teams and four sets of workflows for coffee prep: black, with sugar only, with milk only or with milk and sugar. (For simplicity of exposition, we will disregard different sizes and all the soy, latte, non-fat, decaf, macchiato and suchlike options!) However, even if four teams are organized, they can all follow one central workflow with optional steps depending on customers' stated preferences. We prefer the latter approach for several reasons. To begin with, only one set of workflows has to be maintained. Secondly, all staff are familiar with the overall workflow, even if their team perform some of the individual steps, like adding sugar, and not others, like adding milk. This facilitates cross-training and affords the manager flexibility to make emergency substitutions in staffing if the need arises. Finally, a single workflow with options is much simpler to review—and to explain during audits and operational due diligence meetings.

Workflows go hand-in-hand with policies and procedures. These can range from compliance policies and expense report procedures to information security policies, escalation procedures and business continuity plans. Proper development and documentation of workflows requires knowledge of the policies and procedures in place.

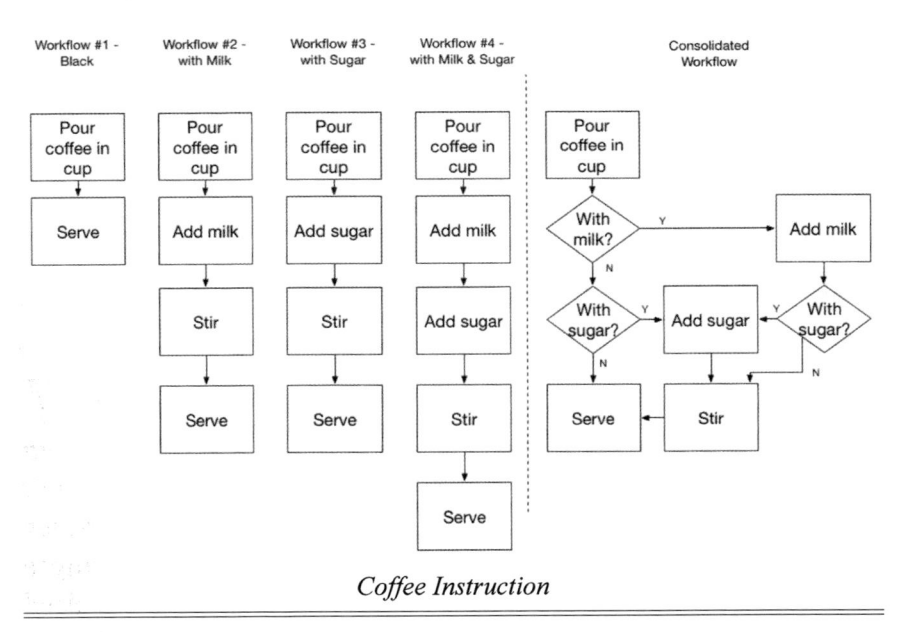

Coffee Instruction

Escalation procedures are worthy of special mention. When things go wrong, as they sometimes will, it is important to have established the criteria and protocols for elevating an issue to a higher level of management. Heads of operations, for example, needn't be informed about every individual reconciliation break or failed trade as it occurs. (They *do* need to see error logs on a regular basis.) Indeed, in larger firms, if they were notified of every single issue, they would be overwhelmed by the volume of small, manageable items and unable to identify whether a major problem is lurking in their e-mailbox. Escalation procedures help by defining which incidents should go up the chain of command and when that should happen. The most effective escalation procedures should use both size and time as decision criteria. For example, a small failed sell transaction may not initially merit escalation due to its size, but should get escalated well before the counterparty issues a buy-in notice. On the other hand, a similar trade that is very large might be escalated immediately because of its size, especially if it is material in relation to the overall portfolio.

Regardless of the state of a firm's documentation, managers must ensure their staff actually follow whatever workflows, policies and procedures have been memorialized. The first step is to confirm that the staff have received copies of the workflows and that they keep them readily at hand. This applies to all the policies, procedures and workflows across the firm, not just to the compliance-related ones. Moreover, asking staff to acknowledge receipt is not good enough. Instead, managers should take steps to ensure their staff read *and understand* these documents. Periodic meetings to review and explain policies, procedures and workflows are a good idea; quizzes may help participants focus. Job swapping, operational reviews and audits can help identify whether workflows are followed.

We like to see workflows available on-line and accessible in the event of a disaster. In a sudden evacuation, you may not have time to collect those reassuringly substantial three-ring binders from your office bookshelf and take them to an offsite location. Yet during a business continuity event, investment managers often must call upon staff to discharge functions they are unaccustomed to performing on a daily basis. It is in exactly these situations when clear, concise, well-documented workflows can be a life-saver.

That's all for now. The coffee is ready!

OPERATIONAL RISK SEVEN
AMALGAMATED ASSIGNMENTS
Improper Segregation of Duties

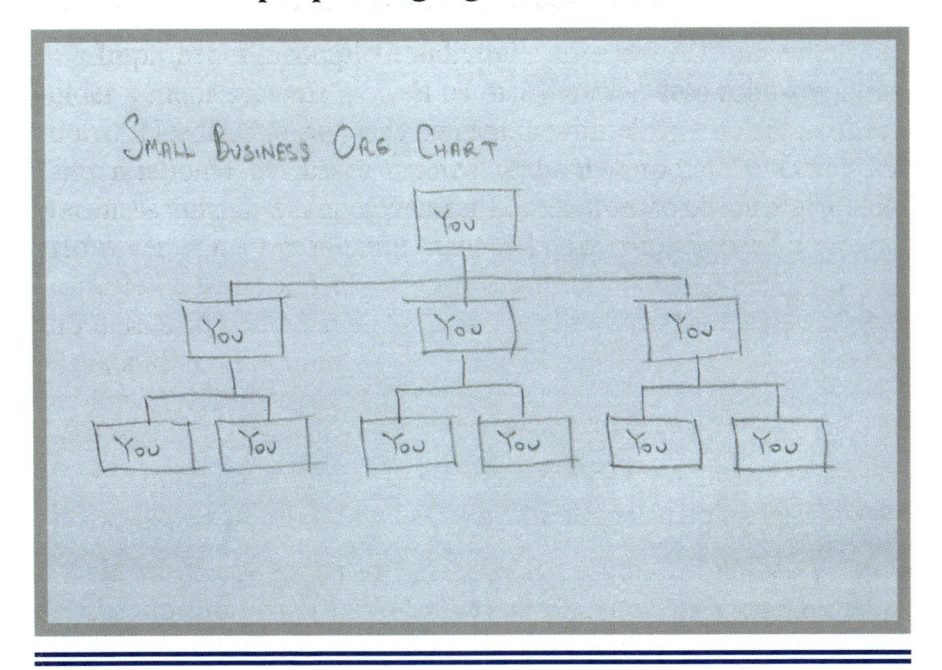

[Hand-drawn organizational chart titled "Small Business Org Chart" showing a hierarchy of boxes all labeled "You"]

WE'RE not writing only about fraud and embezzlement in this chapter. There are other ways in which traditional and alternative investment managers alike, as well as several of their key service providers, suffer from inadequate segregation of duties. And as operational and IT staff were cut back during the financial crisis, this risk area increased in most organizations.

A prevalent source of problems is failing to distinguish, clearly and consistently, between the firm and its clients, particularly when the firm manages commingled accounts. The issue arises with traditional firms managing mutual funds and alternative firms managing hedge funds, private equity funds or funds of hedge funds. Staff with recordkeeping responsibilities often confuse the assets of the *funds* with the assets of the *firm*.

Consider Opaque Asset Management (OAM), which manages the Opaque Fund. It does not matter, for the purpose of this discussion, whether the Opaque Fund is a hedge fund, a private equity fund or a '40 Act mutual fund. Likewise, the fund's strategy is irrelevant.[1] What *is* important is that the Opaque Fund is a *client* of Opaque Asset Management. Indeed, it is quite possible that the fund is OAM's first client, its largest client or both.

But the fund's critically important status as a client is often lost on staff at all levels of the organization. Either they never understood the distinction to begin with or they just forget from time to time. We have seen several instances where senior staff have failed to distinguish between the manager and the fund for so long that they have lost track altogether that a distinction exists. And the common practice of giving the fund a name similar to the firm's increases the likelihood that staff and service providers get muddled.

> **Staff often confuse the assets of the *funds* with the assets of the *firm***

Who cares? To expand on our scenario a bit, let's consider who should be approving wire transfers. Yes, best practice is to have two approvals before release of the transfer. But who should those approving parties be? In many organizations, we see the portfolio managers insist that they approve all wires, but generally they are not the appropriate parties to approve wiring client (i.e., *fund*) assets. Because portfolio managers actually oversee the fund's trading activity, proper segregation of duties would dictate they have no control over the movement of money in and out of the fund. On the other hand, if the portfolio managers are principals of the *investment management firm* and feel strongly they should approve wire

---

[1] Stone House Consulting does not consider a fund type (e.g., hedge fund, mutual fund or private equity fund) to be an asset class or an investment strategy, but rather an investment vehicle. Importantly, we have yet to see anyone employed by a hedge fund *per se*. Instead, staff are employed by a hedge fund manager, a mutual fund manager or a private equity manager.

transfers for the *firm's* money (e.g., payroll, taxes or other major expenses), such a stance is a reasonable approach in most situations. Yet this distinction is commonly overlooked by managers. Indeed, many clients and due diligence firms also fail to pick up on the distinction when reviewing procedures.

This inability to distinguish between the *fund* and the *firm* crops up in other ways as well. Critically important is the issue of books and records, which involves custodians, prime brokers, fund administrators and auditors. Every *fund* will have one or more agents serving as the fund's custodian(s) for the safekeeping of assets. (Hedge funds generally utilize prime brokers who function in several roles, such as execution counterparties, lenders and asset safekeepers/custodians.) Likewise, the fund will have an auditor. Funds also require a fund accountant or fund administrator, which more often than not these days is an external service provider. The custodian, auditor and external fund administrator are hired by the *fund* and not the investment management *firm*. And technically the records maintained by these parties represent the *fund's* (read: *client's*) books and records. They are not the records of the investment management *firm*. So when the regulators walk in for a periodic examination of the *firm*, should Opaque Asset Management rely on client records? We think not.

Separate accounts crystallize the books-and-records issue to an extent. If Opaque Asset Management lands separate account mandates from Pyramid Pension, The Madoff-Stanford Endowment and The City of Ubar, it is problematic for OAM to rely on the books and records produced by *their* agents for the purposes of a regulatory exam. (Separate account clients do not require a fund administrator, so the only book of record would be that of the custodian or prime broker as the safekeeper of assets.) Best practice calls for the investment management firm to maintain its own books and records, generally through the use of an investment accounting system (also known as a portfolio accounting system).

Such an approach is known as *shadow accounting* and allows the manager to have an independent record. Periodic reconciliations serve to identify and resolve discrepancies between manager, safekeeper and, if appropriate, fund administrator records. Commonly used in the traditional investment management arena, shadow accounting represents best practice across the industry.

The issue of shadow accounting is particularly critical when managers evaluate outsourcing. All too often, we hear that traditional and alternative managers have outsourced their middle and back office to a third party which may be a fund administrator and/or a custodian/safekeeper. This puts the third party in the position of fulfilling two roles—first as an extension of the investment manager's operational team and second as a fund administrator or custodian/safekeeper. In a few situations, we have even seen the outsourcing provider act in all three roles as the administrator, the custodian and the manager's middle and back office. In such cases, we like to see the outsourcing provider maintain a different set of books for each role that is played. Failure to maintain separate records certainly streamlines operations because everyone refers to a single record, but the term STP can take on a new meaning—not "straight-through-*processing*" but "straight-through-*problems*."[2]

> Shadow accounting represents best practice across the industry

In addition to distinguishing between firm and fund obligations, investment managers must ensure the activities performed by given individuals or teams do not create conflicts of interest or the potential for theft or fraud. For example, portfolio managers and traders should not price their own portfolios, nor should they be involved in trade settlement or reconciliation. (Recall Nick Leeson or Jérôme Kerviel). Likewise, trade support staff should not perform reconcil-

---

[2] We have seen a number of small investment managers download trade confirmations and upload them to their investment accounting system in lieu of inputting transactions manually or loading them from the manager's trading system. This approach facilitates straight-through-problems as well. If the counterparty's confirmation is incorrect—an all-too-common occurrence for a variety of reasons—then there is no way to catch the mistake. Managers with such a set-up should re-think their process.

iations and vice versa. Performance measurement teams—at least, those responsible for generating performance data for use in marketing and possibly compensation—should not report into the investment team or the sales/marketing area.[3]

When evaluating segregation of duties, managers and those performing due diligence should consider the flow of information as well. We sometimes observe that trade confirmations are sent by counterparties to the trading desk, and the traders, in turn, pass the confirmations on to investment operations. Such an approach provides an opportunity for a trader to alter a confirm. (Messrs. Leeson and Kerviel would have had found this workflow opportune.) We recommend instead that counterparties send confirmations directly to investment operations. If desired, traders can receive copies of the confirmations (or be copied on an email confirm), but they should not be the *conduit* or serve as an intermediary in the delivery process.

Recent downsizing across the industry has left many organizations short-handed. (As an aside, improving the quality of work-life for operational staff has been a recurrent theme in these chapters.) Reductions in force leave fewer people in place to handle the same workload initially and a larger volume of transactions later, as the market recovers before hiring resumes.

> **Due diligence needs to be performed not just once, but on a periodic basis**

Occasionally having too much to do may be energizing, but chronically overextended people, such as those who are covering for their former colleagues, get tired and distracted. They make mistakes.

Think of Barliman Butterbur, the cheerfully scatterbrained landlord in *Lord of the Rings* who tries to hold a conversation—indeed, tries to hold a thought—while serving a large crowd of thirsty hob-

---

[3] For a vigorous discussion of reporting lines for performance measurement teams, please see the CFA Institute webcast, "Firm Management: Where Does Performance Fit?" (available at cfawebcasts.org and on iTunes).

bits and men at the Prancing Pony. "One thing drives out another," he says; "I'm a busy man." Butterbur is unfailingly pleasant and helpful, but many find it hard to remain jovial and optimistic while working at a frantic pace to meet relentless demands. Moreover, serving ale to a customer who called for beer is quickly corrected. The mistakes we make when overtaxed in investment operations may not be so easily unwound.

In some cases, firms that had appropriate segregation controls in place are no longer able to support an approach after workforce reductions. (This illustrates why due diligence needs to be performed not just once, but on a periodic basis.) Other smaller firms, especially start-ups, are challenged simply by the number of people available to perform different functions. Some of these firms may benefit from outsourcing. Others might consider an operational review to identify potential issues and obtain suggestions for remediation.

So who should wire money? It shouldn't be the investment team or anyone involved in reconciliation. Ideally, wire transfers are handled by an internal operations team and two people are required to release a wire. Checks should be put in place to ensure accurate amounts are drawn on the right account and going to the right account. Limiting the specific accounts to which funds can be wired is a sound practice (and, of course, a different group should manage that set-up).

One last thought. You know those little devices your bank or prime broker provides that issue updated codes for initiating wires? Don't leave them in your desk drawer! To begin with, someone else can find them there easily (we almost always do when we conduct an operational review). Secondly, they won't be very helpful in the event you have to invoke your business continuity plan. Inconvenient though it may be, put them on your keychain and take them everywhere!

All that said, we're going to take another look at our own organization chart, job descriptions, workflows and banking authorizations. At the Prancing Pony.

OPERATIONAL RISK EIGHT
RECONCILIATION GAPS
A False Sense of Security

EVERYBODY knows that keeping track of clients' assets is a fundamental responsibility. Everybody also knows that reconciliation—the process of comparing records, identifying and researching discrepancies and, importantly, seeing to it that material errors are *corrected*—is a critical step in satisfying this obligation. It's as simple and obvious as locking the deadbolt on your front door at night. Investment managers employ time-consuming and expensive reconciliation processes and systems to ensure their books and records are accurate, and many readers may be thinking, "We've got it covered. We're in good shape." Yet there are considerations that may not be quite so apparent. This short chapter brings to the surface many of the reconciliation issues we see that have left the best-managed firms more exposed to problems than they realized. We encourage you to take a moment and check whether you also locked the back door.

At a minimum, we expect on the buy side to see reconciliation between the investment manager's records[1] and the safekeeper's records (e.g., the custodian or prime broker). For commingled vehicles such as mutual funds and hedge funds where a fund administrator is required, there should additionally be a reconciliation between the administrator's records and those of the safekeeper. Ideally a three-way reconciliation would take place with a comparison between the administrator's records and the manager's records.[2]

It merits mention here that managers should be aware what really constitutes the safekeeper's records. Many safekeepers will not stand by their electronic representations of an account, but rather consider the paper statement alone to be "official." More importantly, managers that utilize multiple prime brokers to support a given fund may receive consolidated (or "hearsay") reporting from one of those prime brokers showing assets across all the primes servicing the account. In these instances, the firm offering aggregated data to the manager generally is quite clear they are not guaranteeing the accuracy of information on assets not held in custody by them. Consolidating data is unquestionably helpful, but in hearsay reporting the aggregator merely parrots information obtained electronically from the other service providers. We will touch upon this area again in our forthcoming chapter, Operational Risk Nine: Reading the Fine Print.

An effective and complete position reconciliation is not limited to a review of the quantity held on each set of books. Full position reconciliations will examine cost basis and market value in local currency terms. (Tolerances are generally established on these items.) We recommend zero tolerance on quantity and careful exam-

---

[1] If the manager has outsourced investment operations, then we are referring to the third-party provider's investment accounting records.

[2] Commenting on this article after it first appeared, a reader rightly observes that the commonly used phrase "three-way reconciliation" is incorrect. What we have in mind, he suggests, would be more accurately stated as three reconciliations: the investment manager's records vs. the safekeeper's; the safekeeper's vs. the administrator's; and the administrator's vs. the manager's.

ination of fractional shares. In addition, when reconciling quantity on mortgage-backed securities, we suggest reconciling original face amount, particularly since securities trade on that basis.

An oft-neglected item for comparison is the security identifier for each position. There is nothing worse than discovering that rather than owning the class B shares, in actual fact you own the class A shares, or vice versa. Comparison of the security identifier is crucial to make certain you are reviewing the same issue. Where possible, compare the CUSIP for US and Canadian issues and the SEDOL for non-North American securities.[3] Many managers are unaware that an ISIN (International Securities Identifying Number) does not distinguish the market in which a given security was purchased and is held. While it is possible to purchase a security in one market (and pay for it in one currency) and then sell it in another market (possibly receiving proceeds in a second currency), shareholders must take additional steps to convert the shares. So it is important to confirm the security's market denomination. While all will share the same ISIN, the SEDOL number will establish the distinction.

> **We prefer to see managers match 100% of trade tickets to counterparty confirmations**

We also find it necessary to mention that local-currency cash balances must be included in any position reconciliation. If examining trade-date positions, then trade-date cash balances should be used; settlement-date balances should be validated only when reconciling settlement-date positions. Even the most careful reconciliation of a portfolio's holdings is incomplete without concurrently reconciling the portfolio's cash positions. A cash balance that does not reconcile is potentially a sign of other trouble in the portfolio.

A commonplace but critical problem area is the time span be-

---

[3] The acronym CUSIP comes from the Committee on Uniform Security Identification Procedures (1964). SEDOL stands for [London] Stock Exchange Daily Official List.

tween the "as of" date and the date the reconciliation occurs. For example, performing a reconciliation as of 30 September on 1 October—and promptly taking appropriate action to correct errors—is far more effective than performing that same September month-end reconciliation on 25 October. If position breaks remain undiscovered in the interim, managers may be basing investment decisions and compliance monitoring upon incorrect portfolio weights. In addition, managers have increased risk of inadvertently selling short if they hold smaller positions than they suppose.[4] While reconciliation timeframes often are dictated by custodian/prime broker timetables for delivery of reports, automation of the process minimizes the delay.

In some cases it makes sense to reconcile transactions daily. The need for such activity generally depends on several factors, including portfolio turnover, instruments traded and the normal level of cash available. The major drawbacks are twofold. First, daily transaction reconciliations are expensive and time-consuming. Second, reconciliation teams find themselves hunting down what we call "known ghosts" that will disappear of their own accord, such as dividends that the manager credits to cash on pay date but the custodian or prime broker credits one business day later. As a general rule, we prefer to see managers match 100% of trade tickets to counterparty confirmations. This is a reconciliation of sorts. Although it is not the classic manager-to-safekeeper transaction reconciliation typically envisioned, confirmation-matching coupled with careful oversight of external cash flows generally results in an excellent early-warning system for most portfolio activity. Diligently reviewing all position breaks to identify whether they

> Local-currency cash balances must be included in any position reconciliation

---

[4] Obviously, managers could fail to sell enough if they hold larger positions than they think or fail to purchase enough if looking to create or increase a position. But erroneously selling short is particularly concerning because it exposes the portfolio—and therefore the manager—to unlimited potential loss.

resulted from errors on the part of a counterparty, a custodian/prime broker, or the manager will help determine whether more formal daily transaction reconciliations are indicated. If the manager's records are correct most of the time, the need to reconcile transactions every day diminishes.

Managers that trade derivative instruments or have some other reason to have assets held as collateral or margin need to ensure they are receiving statements from the party holding the margin or collateral—and that these statements are the ones used for reconciliation. Simply assuming the clients' assets are held as collateral by the agent without actually hunting down the statement to ensure they were received and are still there is insufficient. In the event of a prime broker failure, a crucial step in claiming collateral that may have been hypothecated (that is, pledged) and re-hypothecated is establishing ownership on the basis of accurate accounting records. Yet not all managers routinely ensure that complete reconciliations are performed. Some have a false sense of security in their belief that they know who has possession of the collateral.

Commissions also belong to the investment manager's clients.[5] There are additional recordkeeping requirements when they are used under commission-sharing arrangements (CSAs) as "soft dollar" payments for research or other products and services supporting the investment decision-making process. Managers who use multiple executing brokers and decision-support providers will have to keep track of numerous cash flows to ensure that soft dollars are being paid as intended. (Here, too, aggregators can be of assistance.) Soft dollar payments are not normally included in a firm's accounting-based reconciliation process but should nonetheless be periodically reviewed somewhere in the organization, for example, by the accounts payable team. Demonstrably sound recordkeeping practices

---

[5] The CFA Institute *Asset Manager Code of Professional Conduct* states that managers "must recognize that commissions paid (and any benefits received in return for commissions paid) are the property of the client." Accordingly, they must "use commissions generated from client trades to pay for only investment related products or services that directly assist the Manager in its investment decision-making process, and not in the management of the firm." (2nd edition, 2010.) Industry best practices can be found in the CFA Institute *Soft Dollar Standards*.

are particularly important in jurisdictions such as the US and the UK where regulations specifically address potential conflicts of interest arising from CSAs.

A widespread reconciliation gap is the absence of a management review confirming that each portfolio was reconciled. Believe it or not, we have seen reconciliation staff duly note breaks but fail to notify anyone of the issue or drop the ball with escalation. (We discussed escalation procedures and criteria in Operational Risk Six: Playbooks.) We have also seen other reconciliation staff simply fail to do their jobs. In addition, sometimes new accounts never get assigned to staff and consequently never get into a reconciliation process. Clearly, a management review is imperative. And when the regulators come to visit, they will seek some sort of proof the review took place. This can be as simple as having the manager who conducted the review initial a reconciliation worksheet or a checklist of the accounts to be reconciled and the date each was completed.

At firms that manage institutional money held in separate portfolios, performance analysts are typically responsible for investigating out-of-tolerance variances between the rates of return calculated by the manager, the custodian and/or the client's investment consultant. This process may provide a final check on the accuracy of data inputs to the return calculations, but it does not remotely constitute a full reconciliation. Performance analysts are not portfolio accountants. They primarily add value in other ways.

One final thought. Trade support staff—and certainly portfolio managers and traders—should not be in the reconciliation business. Aside from protecting firms from fraudulent activity, it generally is difficult to catch one's own ~~typxo's~~ typos.

But it's late. We're going to check *all* the locks, set the alarm, turn off the lights and call it a day.

OPERATIONAL RISK NINE
READING THE FINE PRINT
Know Thy Legal Entities

WE were 45 minutes late for a longstanding engagement yesterday because repairs to an overpass on the highway created an eight-mile traffic jam. We spent the time thinking about the implications—especially for operational managers—of working in a "flow" economy that thrives when people, goods, documents, securities and cash zip from point to point and breaks down when forward movement is impeded. It's an integrated economy that is vulnerable not only to terrorists' attacks on distribution networks but also to the unintended consequences of market participants' high-volume, high-speed activity. Too many drivers, all of them in a hurry, try to squeeze into a single lane and we're late for a meeting. A relatively small and little-known investment manager in the midwestern US fires up an algorithmic trading program, markets around the world drop like a stone and "flash crash" enters the financial lexicon. A major bulge bracket investment bank with a storied history collapses, more than 140,000 trades fail and many hedge funds can't find and retrieve their collateral. Mortgage lenders and servicers disregard the time-consuming legal niceties, foreclosures across the US come to a halt and bank stocks lose value.

Operational disasters occur because, under the pressure of day-to-day work in a high-velocity business, investment managers and their attorneys don't take the time to get things right—to consider all the players in a complex series of transactions, to think through their own firm's processes and controls, and to read the fine print.

We're not lawyers and we presume that you may not be, either. We're all business people, buy-side participants who are more or less expert in a specialized domain of systems and operations. But our lack of training in the law does not exempt us from reading and understanding legal documents, especially contracts, before we sign them. We should not rely exclusively on our attorneys to review a host of business documents such as ISDA, prime brokerage, custodial and administrative agreements—nor should our attorneys allow us to do so. They know securities law, but we know investment operations, technology and client behavior. It takes both groups, lawyers and business people alike, to properly review any agreement and to identify and address the risks.

Significant business issues are often buried within legal documentation. Neither party may intend to obfuscate the terms or conceal the risks. Instead, problems arise because too few qualified and knowledgeable people read the agreement. (Please see Operational Risk Two: The Blind Leading the Blind on ensuring that people know what they are doing.) For example, Bear Stearns used a standard Limited Liability Authority Certificate and Trading Authorization agreement for brokerage accounts. The last full paragraph on the first page laid out what the authorized signatories could do, including among other things trading, receiving confirmations, entering into agreements, wiring funds and even deputizing others to be so authorized. And each signatory

> Significant business issues are often buried within legal documentation

could individually and unilaterally take all these actions.

So what's the problem?

To name but one corollary, signing that document essentially would eliminate, at least as far as Bear Stearns was concerned, any segregation of duties that the manager might have established between trading and settling securities. There would be nothing in place with Bear Stearns to prevent the breach of a manager's internal policy prohibiting a single individual from performing all the listed activities. Yet we have seen managers sign this document without blinking and then reassure investors in due diligence meetings that proper segregation of duties was in place.

Problems like this generally arise when someone in the firm's law department examines an agreement from a legal perspective and those functioning in an operational capacity either do not make it their business to review the document or fail in their responsibility to read it carefully. Moreover, senior managers who execute the document as authorized signatories often follow the "sign here" stickers on the assumption that their subordinates have scrutinized the details. All too often the document is duly placed in a file cabinet, readily available in the event the SEC asks to see it, without having been carefully reviewed by the very people who are responsible for managing the operational risks the agreement may entail. Of course, this bad habit is not limited to operational areas; in our observation, many portfolio managers and financial analysts similarly fail to read prospectuses assiduously before purchasing securities. However, they usually do not fail to include them in their research files for the regulators' benefit. Likewise, simply filing SAS 70 reports without having critically examined them defeats the purpose.

This is how many firms found themselves in trouble during and after the Lehman Brothers bankruptcy,[1] an event that gave new

---

[1] We strongly recommend Alarna Carlsson-Sweeny's excellent article, "Trends in Prime Brokerage," published by Practical Law Company (April 2010). The abstract reads, "This Article considers the shortcomings in the prime brokerage model revealed by the collapse of Lehman Brothers, and examines the contractual issues highlighted by the fallout and the subsequent market response."

meaning to the phrase "collateral damage." In some cases, rather than entering an agreement with Lehman Brothers, Inc. (LBI), investment managers contracted with Lehman Brothers (International) Europe (LBIE), a UK limited liability company. This placed the investment managers' and their clients' assets outside the protections of US bankruptcy courts. In other instances, clients of LBI signed agreements permitting assets to be transferred to LBIE in order to circumvent US re-hypothecation limits. In a book that, despite its tabloid title, should be required reading for every operational manager working in the hedge fund arena, J.S. Aikman summarizes the due diligence facing the administrator of the Lehman Brothers bankruptcy in order to determine who owns the collateral.[2]

In like manner, during the Bear Stearns crisis, many managers discovered that while they enjoyed the legal safeguards created through the use of Bear Stearns Securities Corp. (which insulated prime brokerage assets from a default by Bear Stearns & Co.), they had signed cash sweep agreements that moved excess cash into accounts that ultimately made their fund a general creditor to Bear Stearns & Co.

When assessing counterparty risk, then, not only does a firm need to identify exactly which legal entity is their counterparty, they also have to know the regulators that control that entity. It is, we hope, unnecessary to add that the firm also must continuously monitor its net exposure as well as the entity's creditworthiness. Admittedly, all this isn't easy. It takes state-of-the-art data management, know-how and time. But these days, when investors and regulators are focusing on operational controls and counterparty risk—and calling, too, for improved corporate governance—the burden lies with each of us, in our respective roles, to take responsibility for getting it right.

In that vein, we are going to sit with a cup of coffee and read the proxy statements that our brokers recently sent us. Tomorrow we'll be on the road again. But we'll get an early start because construction crews are working on the highway.

---

[2] J.S. Aikman, *When Prime Brokers Fail: The Unheeded Risk to Hedge Funds, Banks, and the Financial Industry*, Bloomberg Press, An Imprint of Wiley, 2010.

OPERATIONAL RISK TEN
Poor Planning and Slow Response Times
Changes in the Firm, the Marketplace and the Regulatory Environment

"God willing and the creek don't rise" is an expression we sometimes hear in these parts. But two weeks ago the rains did come to the northeastern US. The torrents, which disrupted life on the seaboard from the Carolinas to New England, did not spare the

325-year-old stone house that serves as our firm's headquarters. The first floor was flooded with two to four inches of water.

We're pretty good at strategic planning, operational risk assessment and project management, and we thought we were prepared for heavy weather. We back up our servers in a remote location every night, and our new wing, built to modern architectural standards while respecting the historical character of the property, withstood the floodwaters admirably. In addition, we had moved the computers and Oriental rugs to a contingency site (the second floor), so we were spared considerable inconvenience and expense. But our hastily-developed plan the night before focused too much on indoor assets and failed to consider the outdoor trappings of life and work in the Pennsylvania countryside. We probably couldn't have saved the seemingly solid footbridge over the stream, but we might at least have carried the patio furniture to a safe place.

Neglecting to plan ahead is a fairly obvious source of *business* risk. So why do we mention it in our series on *operational* risk? Because organizations that fail to anticipate future conditions in the marketplace could suddenly find themselves out of business, stranding clients, dislocating employees and damaging shareholders. And because the lack of advance planning can throw operational teams into a frenzy of last-minute activity that turbocharges mistakes. Existing stakeholders deserve better, and—no matter how consistently the firm outperforms the market and its peers—prospective clients and investors will not knowingly allocate assets to organizations whose long-term business prospects are dim or whose ability to keep pace with rapid change is doubtful.

The water is rising fast.

There have been tremendous environmental shifts over the last few years, and the investment management industry is in metamorphosis. Buy-side firms have long been pressured by clients and competitors to offer new investment strategies and products that generate what Laurence B. Siegel calls "true alpha."[1] Now, however, clients and

---

[1] Laurence B. Siegel, "Distinguishing True Alpha from Beta," chapter 25 in Philip Lawton and Todd Jankowski, eds., *Investment Performance Measurement:*

regulators are pressing the industry to increase transparency, provide more timely reporting and information, adopt key industry standards and reduce investment and operational risk. Clients want it all done for lower fees—even as legislators overhaul the financial services framework and newly energized regulators formulate novel requirements. As we urged in an earlier article, "Managing the Business of Asset Management,"[2] managers need more than ever to focus on their own balance sheets and attend to their long-term profitability and survival. In practical terms, that means earnestly considering what lies ahead and mobilizing the resources for effective business planning.

Admittedly, undertaking strategic and operational planning on this scale is daunting, and it's natural to postpone the effort when there are so many urgent and comparatively well-defined issues to resolve from one day to the next. So natural, in fact, and so widespread is the tendency to temporize that highly respected philosophers, psychologists and economists have created an interdisciplinary field of academic research known as "procrastination studies."[3] But the investment management firm and its consultants know the business, read the news, talk to others and see what's happening. In addition, there are well-established techniques such as brainstorming, mind-mapping and forecast calibration[4] that can help the management team survey and evaluate the business risks and structure the planning initiative. Well-defined issues and well-structured problems are more manageable (or at least less intractable).

In most buy-side organizations, staffing represents the largest

---

Evaluating and Presenting Results (Wiley, 2009). Reprinted from *CFA Institute Conference Proceedings: Challenges and Innovation in Hedge Fund Management* (July 2004).

[2] Available at articles.stonehouseconsulting.com.

[3] See James Surowiecki's review article, "Later: What Does Procrastination Tell Us About Ourselves?" in *The New Yorker* (October 11, 2010).

[4] Douglas W. Hubbard, whose writing we admire, explains calibrating one's forecasting ability in *How to Measure Anything: Finding the Value of Intangibles in Business*, 2nd edition (Wiley, 2010) and *The Failure of Risk Management: Why It's Broken and How to Fix It* (Wiley, 2009).

single category of expense. Even with political and market pressure to reduce Wall Street compensation, investment managers will still find that the cost of talent tops the list of annual expenditures. Yet failure to anticipate staffing costs and manage them proactively, especially in intermediate- and long-term business plans, is commonplace. In good part, this breakdown arises from the disconnect between the key driver for increased revenues (assets under management or AUM) and the key driver for increased costs (the number of accounts managed). Too many business projections focus solely on AUM growth without regard to the underlying account growth that impels increases in staffing as well as systems and, of course, operational risk.

Operational benchmarking can assist firms in analyzing their cost structure and quantifying the monetary impact of changes in key drivers.[5] However, having failed to base their business plans upon the right measures, many firms then fail a second time by not reinvesting in their organizations in advance of growth. It is only when service quality indicators, such as the timeliness and accuracy of client reporting, begin to slip in the aftermath of significant business expansion that many organizations finally address their inadequate staffing or infrastructure. In some cases, this lack of planning results in band-aid solutions that are described as temporary measures but, due to the unending stream of burning issues to resolve, become permanent fixtures over time. (See above: procrastination.) Workarounds become the order of the day. Staff get overstretched. Operational risk soars.

> Poor planning is often manifest in the new product launch process

Poor planning is often manifest in the new product launch process, which we have previously mentioned in connection with training (Operational Risk Three: Novices, Apprentices and Soloists)

---

[5] Stone House Consulting and its strategic partner, Investit, offer operational benchmarking services and tools for investment management organizations. Please visit stonehouseconsulting.com for further information.

and workflow documentation (Operational Risk Six: Playbooks). Inaugurating a new investment strategy or fund requires significant planning and conscientious communication. Whether in the interest of secrecy or the rush to bring offerings to market, firms often wait until the last minute to notify operations or technology staff of strategic decisions. But it takes time—and, again, careful planning—to ensure adequate workflows, procedures and systems are in place to support the new initiative. In many instances, the problems arise from surprise investments in new markets or instruments that may require unforeseen systems changes; extra set-up with the affected custodians, prime brokers and administrators; additional valuation policies and pricing sources; and new client and regulatory reporting. As a rule, the more advance notice given, the fewer the operational problems.

Best-practice firms have new product committees that meet on a regular basis to discuss, review and approve all new product launches, including the utilization of new types of investment vehicles (separate accounts, hedge funds, etc.). Compliance, operations and IT staff actively participate in these committees. They are not merely recipients of a memo or an e-mail informing them late in the game about what is coming, nor, worse still, do they discover new security types or investment in new markets after the fact.

In addition to focusing on strategic moves that are, to some degree, within the investment manager's control, the most forward-looking firms will consider external factors. One obvious area where such planning is required is business continuity or disaster recovery. Less obvious, but no less important, are emerging developments in the market and regulatory environment.

We see a wave of changes coming.

While the Dodd-Frank Act has passed in the US, and we have a pretty good idea which agencies and regulators will implement its provisions, many of the details have yet to be revealed. CFA Institute,[6] the Council of Institutional Investors,[7] and other organiza-

---

[6] cfainstitute.org

[7] cii.org

tions have studied aspects of this comprehensive legislation, and we won't attempt to improve on their analyses. We will limit ourselves to a few observations about the likely impact on buy-side firms.

First, we know that many more alternatives managers—including firms that are not domiciled within the US—will have to register with the Securities and Exchange Commission. (Still others will have to contend with regulatory requirements at the state level, much as insurance companies have done for many years.) Registration will necessitate implementing and documenting a significant number of policies and procedures for many managers. Second, to comply with voluminous reporting requirements imposed by clients and regulators, we know that investment managers must harness their data to satisfy new demands for transparency. Third, we know that all these additional regulatory requirements will cost money. This is likely to result in significant merger-and-acquisition activity and outsourcing across the industry, as firms that are already under margin pressure try to leverage their infrastructure by achieving greater scale (read: more AUM without a proportionate increase in staffing). The barriers to entry are rising and will stay high. Smaller firms that are not acquired will struggle to survive.

In addition to regulatory reform, we see clients continuing to apply pressure on investment managers, in large part because of the pressures *they* are under. Institutional investors—especially but not exclusively pension plan sponsors—must own up to their unfunded liabilities and will relentlessly hammer managers for higher returns and lower fees.

We also foresee that, as M&A activity accelerates, the line between traditional and alternative managers will blur and the two standards of care that currently prevail in the institutional marketplace will come together. Bear with us; this is important. When selecting external managers today, institutional investors and their consultants require traditional firms (but not hedge funds) to comply with the Global Investment Performance Standards (GIPS®)[8] and subject hedge funds (but not traditional managers) to intensive

---

[8] gipsstandards.org

operational due diligence (ODD). Convergence is inevitable. We strongly encourage hedge funds to implement the GIPS® standards[9] and traditional managers to prepare for ODD. Many organizations with superior leadership are already performing operational reviews, documenting their workflows, developing IT roadmaps and reviewing their approach to outsourcing and managing external service providers.

But here's the good news: rising client expectations and heightened regulatory oversight will prompt senior management to place greater emphasis on operational excellence through best-practice processes, improved data management, more effective controls and appropriate investment in staff and infrastructure. As the market improves and growth resumes, forward-looking firms will re-examine the organizational structure and develop smart staffing and technology plans to have enough employees with the right skills without recreating the jobs that were so painful to eliminate during the market crisis. At the same time, margin pressure will drive further technological improvements and outsourcing to increase scalability, improve quality and control costs.

Meanwhile, we found our footbridge about half a mile downstream. Mindful of our own limitations, we watched seasoned contractors re-install it this week while we read the financial press in our new patio chairs. This one should last. God willing and the creek don't rise.

---

[9] See ACA Compliance Group's 2010 white paper, "Compliance Is Easier Than You Think: Challenges and Solutions for Hedge Fund Managers Considering the Global Investment Performance Standards (GIPS®)," available at acacompliancegroup.com/documents/ACA Beacon Hedge Fund White Paper.pdf.

Conclusion

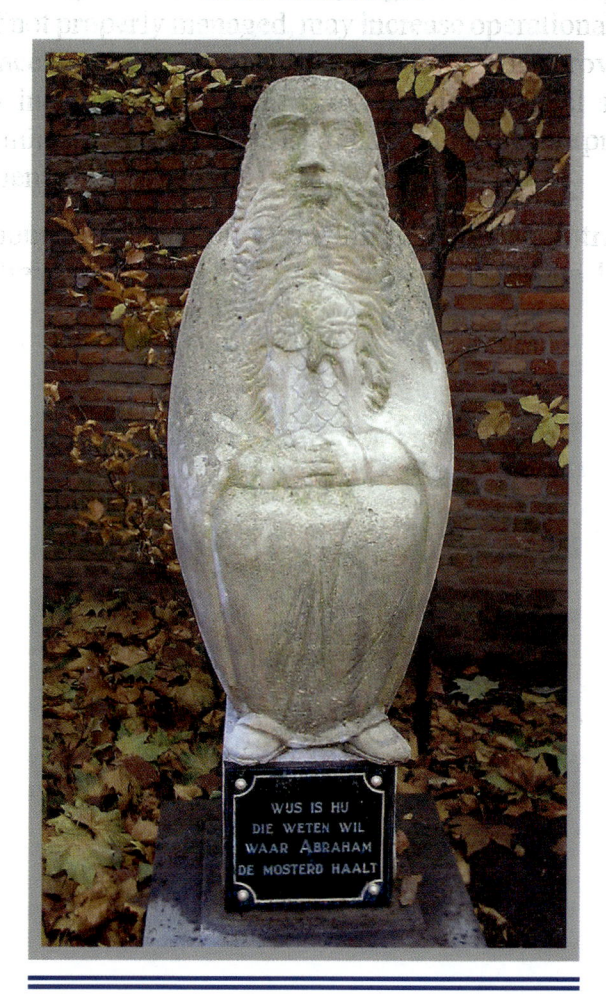

THERE'S an old Dutch or Flemish proverb that says, "Wise is he who wants to know where Abraham gets the mustard."[1] The refer-

---

[1] *"Wijs is hij die weten wil waar Abraham de mosterd haalt."* The word mustard (*mosterd*) is a corruption of another word (*mutsaard*) that means a fagot, that is, a bundle of sticks and branches bound together. Thus the proverb might be more loosely translated, "Wise is the one who wants to know where Abraham gets the firewood." The reference is to a Biblical text: "Abraham took the wood for the burnt offering, loaded it on Isaac, and carried in his own hands the fire and the knife." (Gen. 22-6.) The accompanying photograph shows a statue standing on a

ence to Abraham's mustard is rather obscure, but with a little research we learned that, like many traditional sayings, this one contains a valuable truth. It means, "Wise is the one who wants to know how things are done."

Managing investment operations can be a thankless job. In many organizations, senior management is blithely unaware of what it takes to design, implement, maintain and upgrade the systems and workflows that support the business from account set-up through client reporting across a range of investment strategies, markets and instruments. It is understandable that middle- and back-office supervisors and employees may feel they are noticed only when things go wrong. And if their department is understaffed they may think they'll never get ahead of the flow of transactions long enough to engineer the system changes, workflow improvements or additional controls that might streamline processes, reduce error rates and mitigate the reputational risk to which the firm as a whole and they as individuals are exposed.

In these short chapters, we have attempted to survey major areas and sources of buy-side operational risk and suggest ways in which firms might address them. Here are some of the lessons:

1. Evidence of complacency can be found in flawed business continuity plans, poor recordkeeping and deficient insurance coverage. Other practices that place organizations at risk are hiring inexperienced or under-qualified staff, neglecting to train new employees, disregarding feedback from middle- and back-office staff, operating without an electronic document management system and failing to check employees' work.

2. Mid-level and senior managers who are unfamiliar with investment operations may rely upon subordinates who are also unqualified for the task at hand. Hiring, promoting and coaching people who demonstrate both leadership and technical skills can improve the likelihood that department heads are well-equipped to manage operations, and external operational reviews can as-

---

pedestal with a plaque that bears the proverb. The statue is in St. Donatus Park, Leuven, Belgium.

sist with determining whether there are organizational risks. Outsourcing does not relieve an organization of responsibility and, if not properly managed, may increase operational risk. Due diligence in selecting and monitoring key service providers minimally includes issuing RFPs, examining financial statements, performing periodic onsite visits and reading the fine print in legal documents.

3. Thoughtful attention to organizational design, training and cross-training can promote teamwork and reduce key-person risk at all levels. Forming small, specialized teams fosters isolation, may result in an unnecessarily high number of workflows and leaves the firm exposed to the loss of intellectual capital and institutional knowledge. The presence of soloists—individuals who assume sole responsibility for a function or client relationship and jealously guard their domain—is a warning sign. Training resources include conferences, live and online classes and short courses, and internal "lunch-and-learn" sessions.

4. Hand-offs between people, departments, organizations and systems are fraught with communication and timing challenges. Most useful for identifying potential trouble spots are system diagrams that identify all applications and their interfaces, and workflow diagrams that display hand-offs between teams or departments and between the firm and external counterparties, service providers and clients.

5. Automation is frequently the best approach to mitigating operational risk. However, it is essential to keep system access permissions up-to-date, ensure that complete and accurate audit trails are built in and maintain the systems infrastructure. Successful project teams include experienced buy-side staff and/or consultants who know how to perform the activities manually and understand the operational context (i.e., the system and workflow linkages). Consultants should have a plan for transferring knowledge to the firm's staff during the project.

6. Inexistent, obsolete or incomplete process-and-procedure documentation is frequently a factor in operational breakdowns.

Minimally customized workflow diagrams that are kept up-to-date and readily available are useful in new-hire training, system- and process-improvement initiatives and disaster recovery. Escalation protocols should take into account both size and time.

7. When designing organizational structures, policies and procedures for the segregation of duties, it is vitally important to maintain the distinction between the firm and the fund(s) it manages. Shadow accounting enables investment management firms to have their own books and records for comparison with those of custodians, auditors and external fund administrators. Operational reviews can help firms ensure that the activities performed by individuals or teams do not create conflicts of interest or the potential for theft or fraud.

8. Firms are well advised to conduct full reconciliations between their records and those of the custodians and administrators and to have supervisors review and initial them. Full reconciliations include comparisons of cost basis and market value in local currency terms, security identifiers and local-currency cash balances. Firms must also take care to reconcile margin or collateral positions using statements from the party holding the assets. Performance analysts who investigate out-of-tolerance variances in rates of return provide a final check on the accuracy of input data, but this activity is not the same as a full reconciliation.

9. Legal documents should be reviewed in detail not only by the firm's attorneys but also by knowledgeable operational managers. When assessing counterparty risk, firms need to identify exactly which legal entity is their counterparty, determine who has regulatory jurisdiction and continuously monitor net exposures and the counterparty's creditworthiness.

10. The investment management industry is in flux, and organizations that fail to plan ahead are at risk. Clients are pressing firms to increase transparency, provide more timely reporting, adopt key industry standards, reduce investment and operational risk and lower their advisory fees even as regulatory requirements grow. Operational benchmarking can assist firms in analyzing their cost structure and quantifying the monetary impact of changes in key drivers. The line between traditional and alternative managers will blur; the former are encouraged to prepare for operational due diligence and the latter, to implement the GIPS standards.

We earnestly hope that this collection of chapters will contribute, however modestly, to a new culture of excellence in firm management. The strongest firms will be those with senior managers who want to know how things are done, appreciate the knowledge and experience of superior operational staff, give them the resources they need to mitigate risks, excuse them for events beyond their reasonable control and reward them for their successful efforts to keep the complex machinery of investment management running smoothly.

APPENDIX
Mitigating Lottery Risk[1]

WHAT would happen to your firm, or your investment operations group—or you as the manager of the affected department—if the only person who knows how to perform a vital function were to win this week's lottery…and resign?

Surely you would celebrate your key employee's good fortune no less than, say, your grandfather's 100th birthday. However, you'd probably also experience that free-fall sensation you get whenever you know that something bad is going to happen. (Recall the moment you realised that someone reporting to you had made a terrible mistake and you'd have to tell senior management what happened.) Lottery risk, just like longevity risk, is the downside of a good thing. You might congratulate your employee, or your grandfather, but decline a piece of cake. Grandfather has outlived his assets. How will you pay for his assisted living and health care? Diana has left the firm. How will you produce the month-end client reports?

Every firm and every department is more or less exposed to the sudden, unexpected departure of key people. Lottery risk used to be known as the danger of someone getting hit by a bus or a beer truck, and accordingly many firms have key-person life insurance on their

---

[1] ©Osney Media 2010. Reprinted by permission. This article originally appeared in *Performance Measurement and Client Reporting Review*, Vol. 3.1, Autumn 2010.

C-level executives. More to the point, the fundamentals of sound managerial practice include the requirements to document processes and procedures and to train backup personnel in functions critical to ongoing operations and client service. Everybody knows this—it's just common sense—and everybody agrees, in principle, that documentation and cross-training cannot be neglected.

You are hardly alone, however, if your department's training efforts are haphazard and your workflow documentation is missing, obsolete or otherwise defective. All too few operating units are adequately prepared for the loss of a key trading system administrator, portfolio accountant or investment performance analyst. Let's consider, in particular, why process-and-procedure documentation may not be done, or may not be done very well. Once we have identified the obstacles, we can see how to surmount them.

Documentation impediments to overcome

In general, operations are undocumented or poorly documented due to a lack of time, motivation and expertise.

The first impediment, the lack of time, is real, serious, unhealthy and probably getting worse as firms strive to offset margin pressure by "doing more with less". Many good men and women are in action nonstop from the moment they reach their workplace until the time, some 10 or more hours later, when they are free to leave or too dog-tired to continue. Lunch may be a deli salad or a vending-machine candy bar, and dinner is take-away. The only rest they get is on a commuter train. Merely keeping pace with transactions takes everything they've got. Documenting processes is out of the question. Not this week.

The great steel mills in western Pennsylvania used to shut down for maintenance every summer. During a two-week period engineers, mechanics and labourers would reline the blast furnaces, overhaul the machinery, and attend to all the other tasks that could not be accomplished when the mill is in production. Most of the workers would take a holiday.

There are no such scheduled plant closings in the investment management business, where the capital markets are always open somewhere and firms pass the book from one trading desk to another. Nonetheless, as the departmental manager, you may be aware of relative lulls. For instance, there may be fewer service demands in the middle of the second month after quarter-end. Accordingly, it may be possible to dedicate one or two particular weeks every year (preferably off-season so as to work around staff holidays) to creating or updating process-and-procedure documentation.

There is always something more urgent or more interesting than maintaining documentation, but employees' lack of motivation is somewhat easier to manage than the demands on their time. Staff members should be made explicitly accountable for the usefulness and accuracy of operational documentation in their area of expertise and managers should evaluate their performance in this domain. In other words, just as managers take into account the employee's knowledge of the job, teamwork, productivity and the like, they should consider the employee's success in keeping useful documentation up-to-date when they make and explain decisions about compensation.

The remaining obstacle, a lack of expertise in the techniques of workflow analysis and documentation, may be the easiest to overcome. In large organisations the training department might offer a short course (and they would most likely be thrilled if an operating manager were to ask for their assistance), or a corporate office might make an internal consultant available. There may be low-cost online courses. Alternately, the firm could call upon an external consultant with experience in documenting investment operations. As long as the manager understands that a consultant-led project requires the cooperative attention of key staff, this can be a highly effective approach.

Without being cavalier about the foregoing impediments, let's suppose that you've found the time, motivated the staff and lined up pertinent expertise in the person of a qualified researcher. You are ready to bring your process-and-procedure documentation up to your own standards. Others have reached this promising stage but have not proceeded to achieve results. What goes wrong? Why isn't documentation done very well?

The Karmarkar gambit

In 1984 Narendra Karmarkar, at the time a mathematician employed by AT&T's Bell Labs, invented and announced an algorithm to solve complex linear programming problems far more powerfully and efficiently than the widely-used simplex method. When other mathematicians were unable to corroborate Karmarkar's technique, however, they vigorously called his work and even his moral character into question. It subsequently came to light that Bell Labs had withheld critical steps in order to develop and patent commercial applications in advance of the competition.

The case raises fascinating questions about science and business because the one rests upon openness to testing and the other has a legitimate interest in protecting intellectual property. In the context of organizational behaviour, "the Karmarkar gambit" can be seen in action whenever business units or individual staff members appear to be engaged, but actually hold back vital information in an understandable but wrong-headed attempt to protect their position.

The Karmarkar gambit and similar tactics are symptomatic of attitudes that are hard to elicit, much less change. The employee may feel that the process in question is their own private property and that they have to keep trespassers at bay. At a deeper level they may be driven by a concern for job security; after all, people they love are dependent upon their income, and they may very well have acquaintances who have been unemployed for many months. It might help to let the employee know that they are valued and that documenting the operations for which they are responsible (and, in due time, training backup personnel) may make them eligible for more challenging, better-paid positions. They certainly cannot be considered for a promotion as long as nobody else knows their job.

And get some sleep...

Chronic fatigue makes it even harder to deal with the relentless demands of a manager's job and other commitments. You may sleep more easily and soundly if you take steps to mitigate the risks that are at least partially under your control. Financial planning may help you care for your grandfather, and there is a simple, pedestrian means of reducing lottery risk: get your processes and procedures properly documented, and cross-train your staff on one another's jobs. Then you can celebrate everyone's good fortune without reservation.

About Stone House Consulting, LLC

Established amid market turmoil in 2008, Stone House Consulting provides strategic, operational and IT advisory services, benchmarking and implementation support to traditional and alternative investment management organizations. Stone House Consulting also conducts industry research and practice-oriented training programs.

Holly Miller, founding partner, and Philip Lawton, partner, are well known for their speaking and writing in the areas of investment operations, outsourcing and performance measurement. With more than 60 years of buy-side experience between them, Ms. Miller and Mr. Lawton have assisted the world's leading investment managers on a variety of change initiatives and cross-divisional projects throughout their careers.

In 2010 Stone House Consulting and Investit Ltd. announced a strategic partnership allowing both firms to offer one another's products and services to their increasingly global clientele. Investit's offices in London, Sydney and Dubai complement Stone House Consulting's coverage of the US from their headquarters in the Philadelphia/Wilmington area.

For more information on Stone House Consulting, please visit the firm's website at http://www.stonehouseconsulting.com.

Made in the USA
Lexington, KY
12 April 2011